FERBANE

AUG 2023

WITHDRAWN

PUPPY VERSUS KITTEN

OFFALY LIBRARY	
30013005163990	
Bertrams	43/1
741.5941	
DC	0229813

ANDY RILEY IS THE AUTHOR/ARTIST OF A WHOLE LOAD OF CARTOON BOOKS:
THE BOOK OF BUNNY SUICIDES, DAWN OF THE BUNNY SUICIDES,
RETURN OF THE BUNNY SUICIDES, GREAT LIES TO TELL SMALL KIDS,
LOADS MORE LIES TO TELL SMALL KIDS, SELFISH PIGS,
WINE MAKES MUMMY CLEVER, BEER MAKES DADDY STRONG,
D.I.Y. DENTISTRY (AND OTHER ALARMING INVENTIONS), AND ROASTED.

HIS ONGOING KING FLASHYPANTS CHILDREN'S BOOK SERIES INCLUDES:
KING FLASHYPANTS AND THE EVIL EMPEROR,
KING FLASHYPANTS AND THE CREATURE FROM CRONG,
AND KING FLASHYPANTS AND THE TOYS OF TERROR.

HE'S AN EMMY-WINNING SCRIPTWRITER WHOSE CREDITS INCLUDE:
VEEP, BLACK BOOKS, LITTLE BRITAIN, GNOMEO & JULIET,
TRACEY ULLMAN'S SHOW, THE ARMANDO IANNUCCI SHOWS,
SPITTING IMAGE, THE FRIDAY NIGHT ARMISTICE, HYPERDRIVE,
THE GREAT OUTDOORS, BIG TRAIN, THE BOY IN THE DRESS,
GANGSTA GRANNY, COME FLY WITH ME, ARMSTRONG AND MILLER
AND ROBBIE THE REINDEER.

MISTERANDYRILEY.COM

TWITTER: @andyrileyish

PUPPY VERSUS KITTEN

Andy RiLey

FIRST PUBLISHED IN GREAT BRITAIN IN 2017 BY HODDER & STOUGHTON
AN HACHETTE UK COMPANY

3

COPYRIGHT © ANDY RILEY 2017

THE RIGHT OF ANDY RILEY TO BE IDENTIFIED AS THE AUTHOR OF THE WORK HAS BEEN
ASSERTED BY HIM IN ACCORDANCE WITH THE COPYRIGHT, DESIGN AND PATENTS ACT 1988.

ALL RIGHTS RESERVED. NO PART OF THIS PUBLICATION MAY BE REPRODUCED, STORED
IN A RETRIEVAL SYSTEM, OR TRANSMITTED, IN ANY FORM OR BY ANY MEANS
WITHOUT THE WRITTEN PERMISSION OF THE PUBLISHER, NOR BE OTHERWISE
CIRCULATED IN ANY FORM OF BINDING OR COVER OTHER THAN THAT IN WHICH
IT IS PUBLISHED AND WITHOUT A SIMILAR CONDITION BEING IMPOSED ON THE
SUBSEQUENT PURCHASER.

A CIP CATALOGUE RECORD FOR THIS TITLE IS AVAILABLE FROM THE BRITISH LIBRARY

ISBN 978 0 340 99794 9
EBOOK ISBN 978 1 444 728156

PRINTED AND BOUND IN GREAT BRITAIN BY CPI GROUP (UK) LTD, CROYDON, CRO 4YY

HODDER & STOUGHTON POLICY IS TO USE PAPERS THAT ARE NATURAL, RENEWABLE AND
RECYCLABLE PRODUCTS AND MADE FROM WOOD GROWN IN SUSTAINABLE FORESTS.
THE LOGGING AND MANUFACTURING PROCESSES ARE EXPECTED TO CONFORM TO THE
ENVIRONMENTAL REGULATIONS OF THE COUNTRY OF ORIGIN.

HODDER & STOUGHTON LTD.
CARMELITE HOUSE
50 VICTORIA EMBANKMENT
LONDON EC4Y ODZ

WWW. HODDER. CO.UK

WITH THANKS TO

HANNAH BLACK, GORDON WISE, IAN WONG,
NIALL HARMAN, RICHARD PIKE, KEVIN CECIL,
BILL RILEY, EDDIE RILEY

AND

POLLY FABER

DEDICATED TO

DAVID AYRES

LOOK! THEY'RE MAKING FRIENDS.
WHAT is THAT
WHAT is THAT

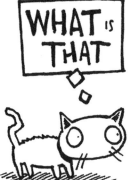

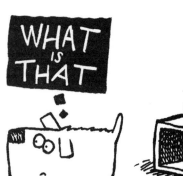

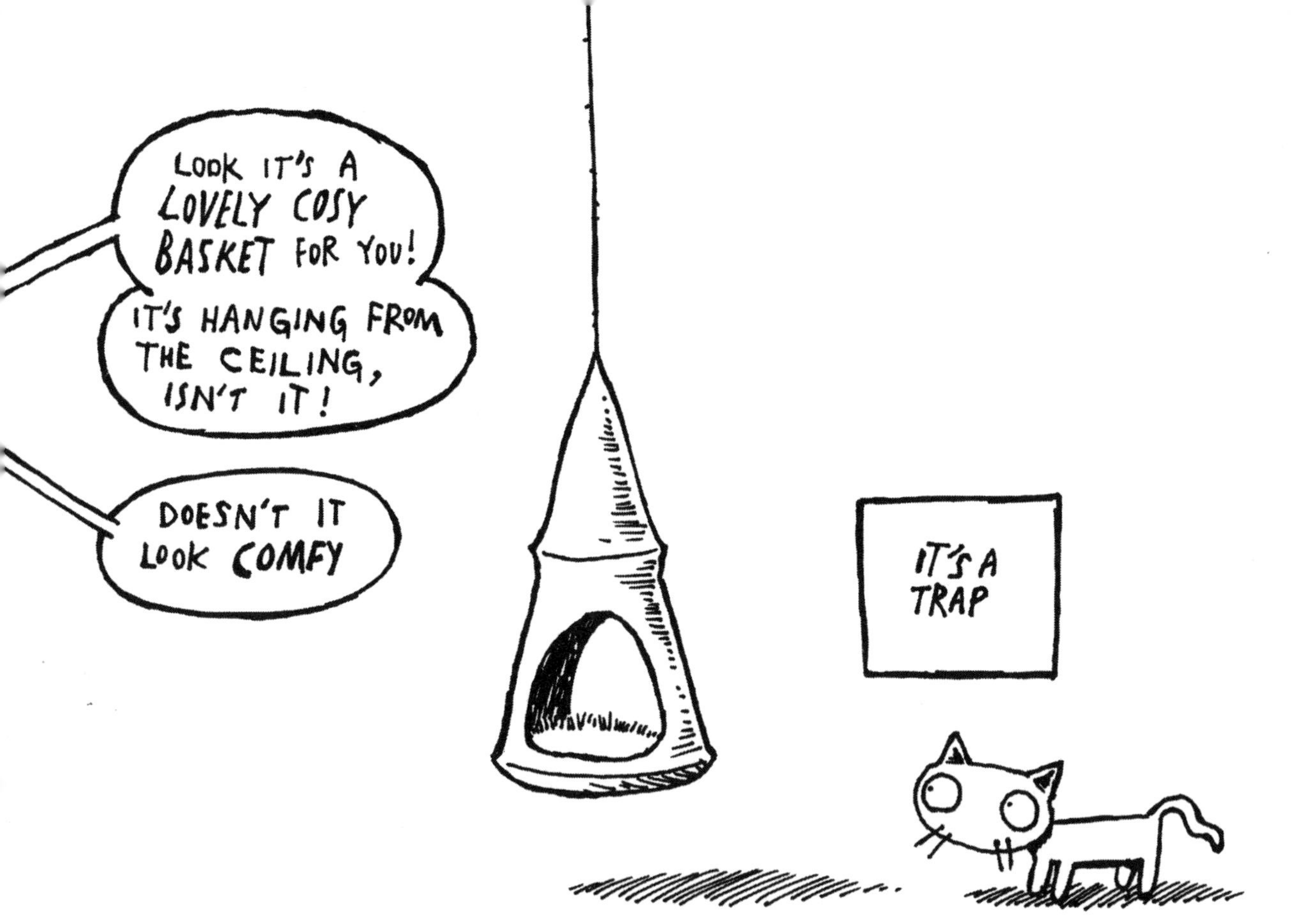
LOOK IT'S A LOVELY COSY BASKET FOR YOU!
IT'S HANGING FROM THE CEILING, ISN'T IT!
DOESN'T IT LOOK COMFY
IT'S A TRAP

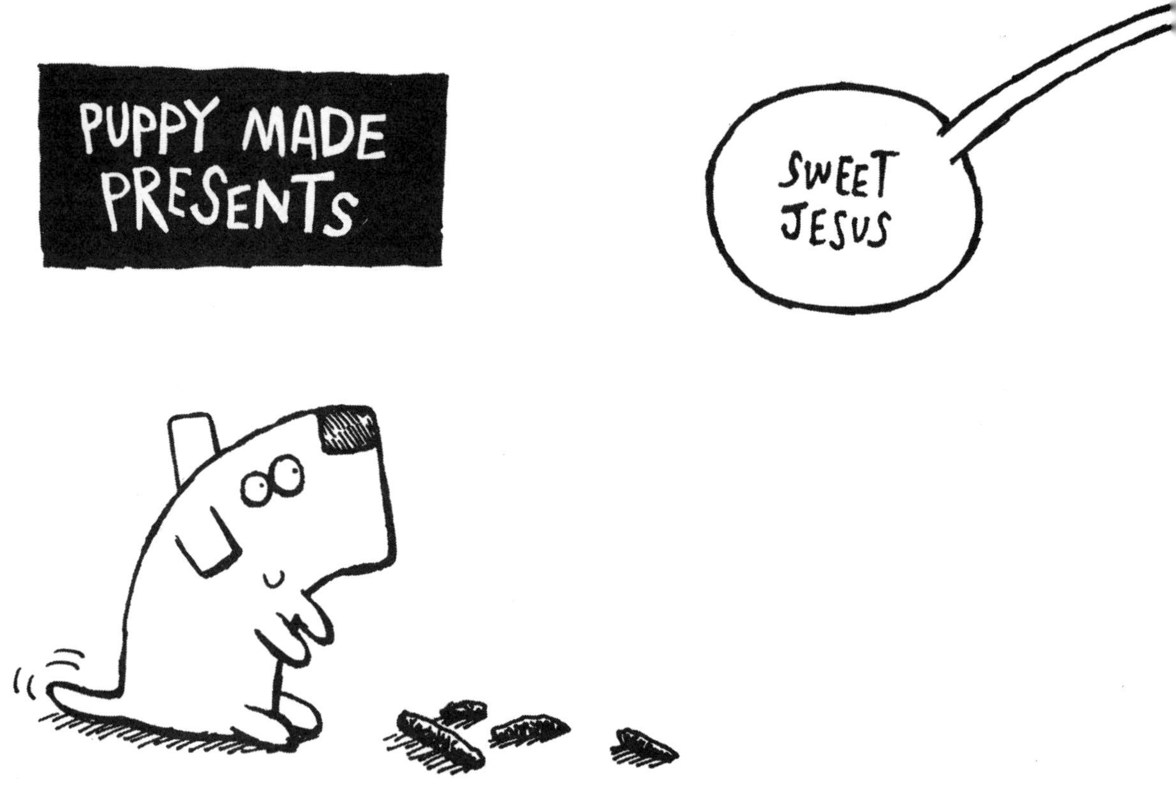
PUPPY MADE PRESENTS
SWEET JESUS

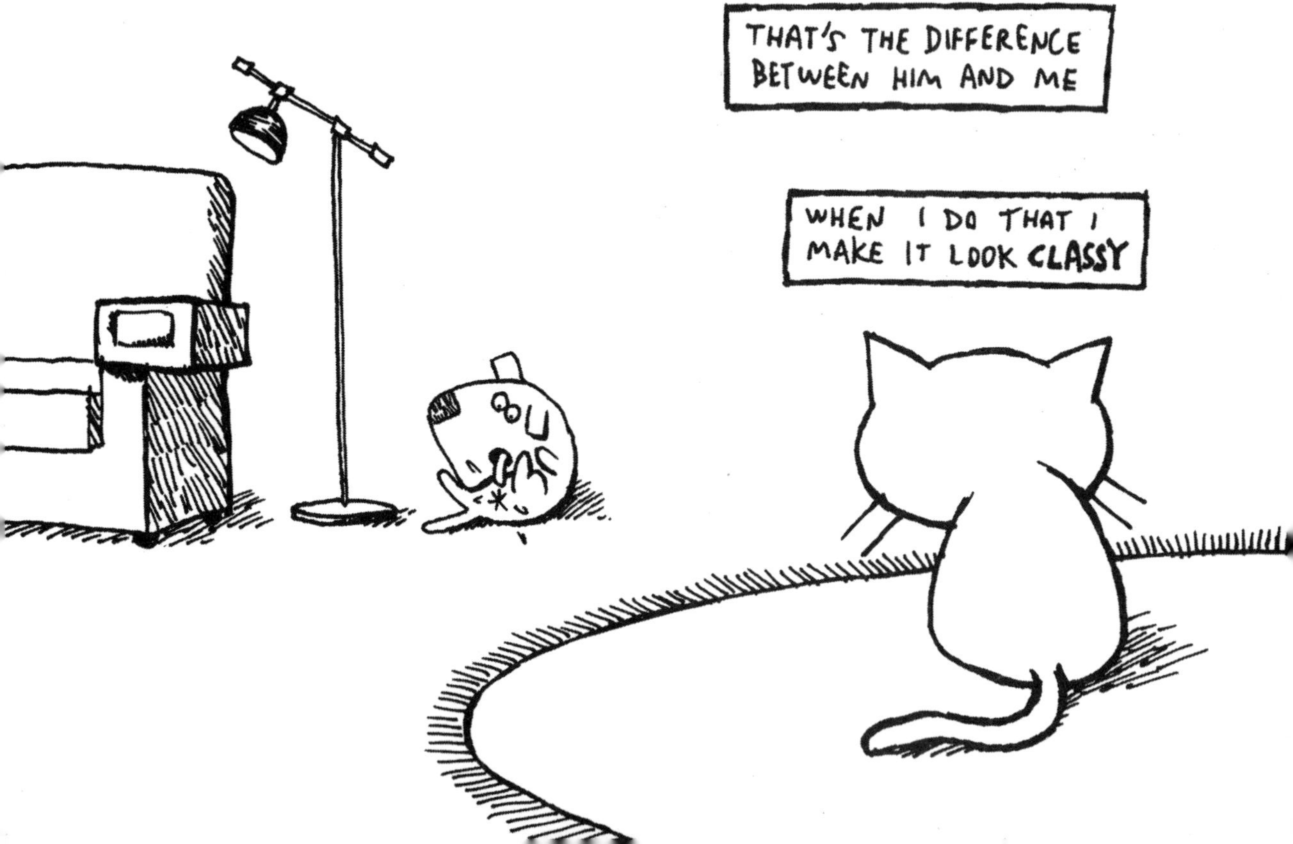
THAT'S THE DIFFERENCE BETWEEN HIM AND ME
WHEN I DO THAT I MAKE IT LOOK CLASSY

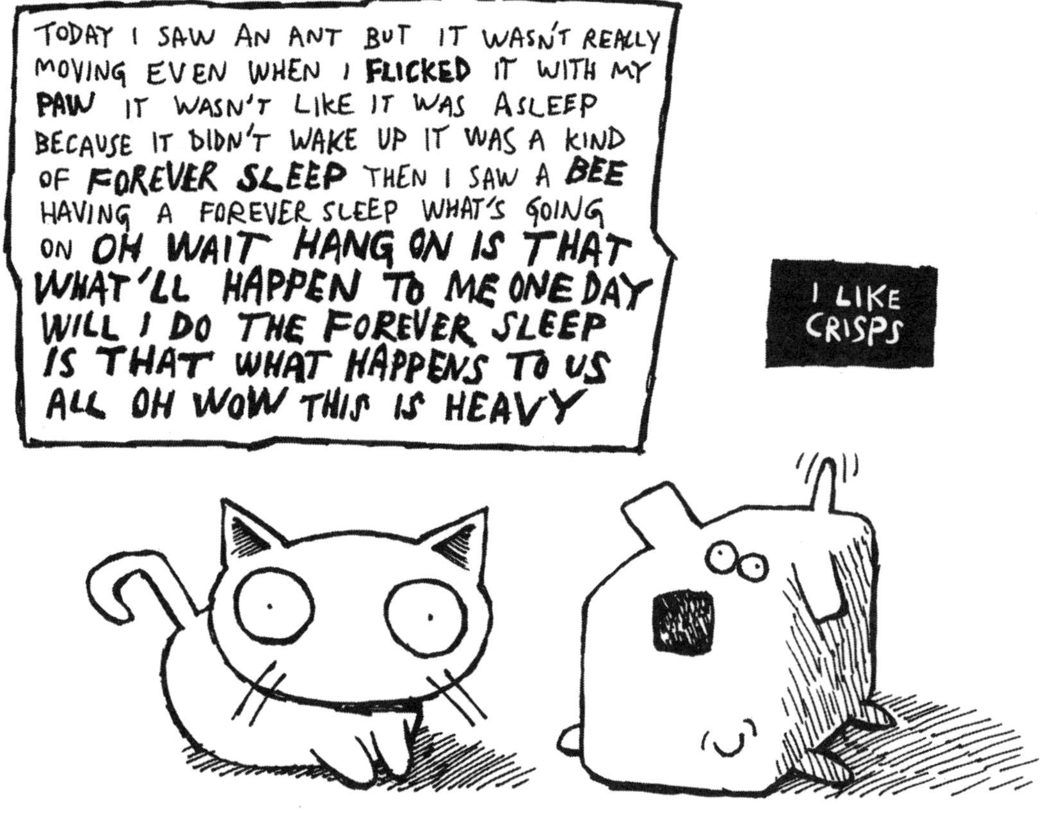
TODAY I SAW AN ANT BUT IT WASN'T REALLY MOVING EVEN WHEN I FLICKED IT WITH MY PAW IT WASN'T LIKE IT WAS ASLEEP BECAUSE IT DIDN'T WAKE UP IT WAS A KIND OF FOREVER SLEEP THEN I SAW A BEE HAVING A FOREVER SLEEP WHAT'S GOING ON OH WAIT HANG ON IS THAT WHAT'LL HAPPEN TO ME ONE DAY WILL I DO THE FOREVER SLEEP IS THAT WHAT HAPPENS TO US ALL OH WOW THIS IS HEAVY
I LIKE CRISPS

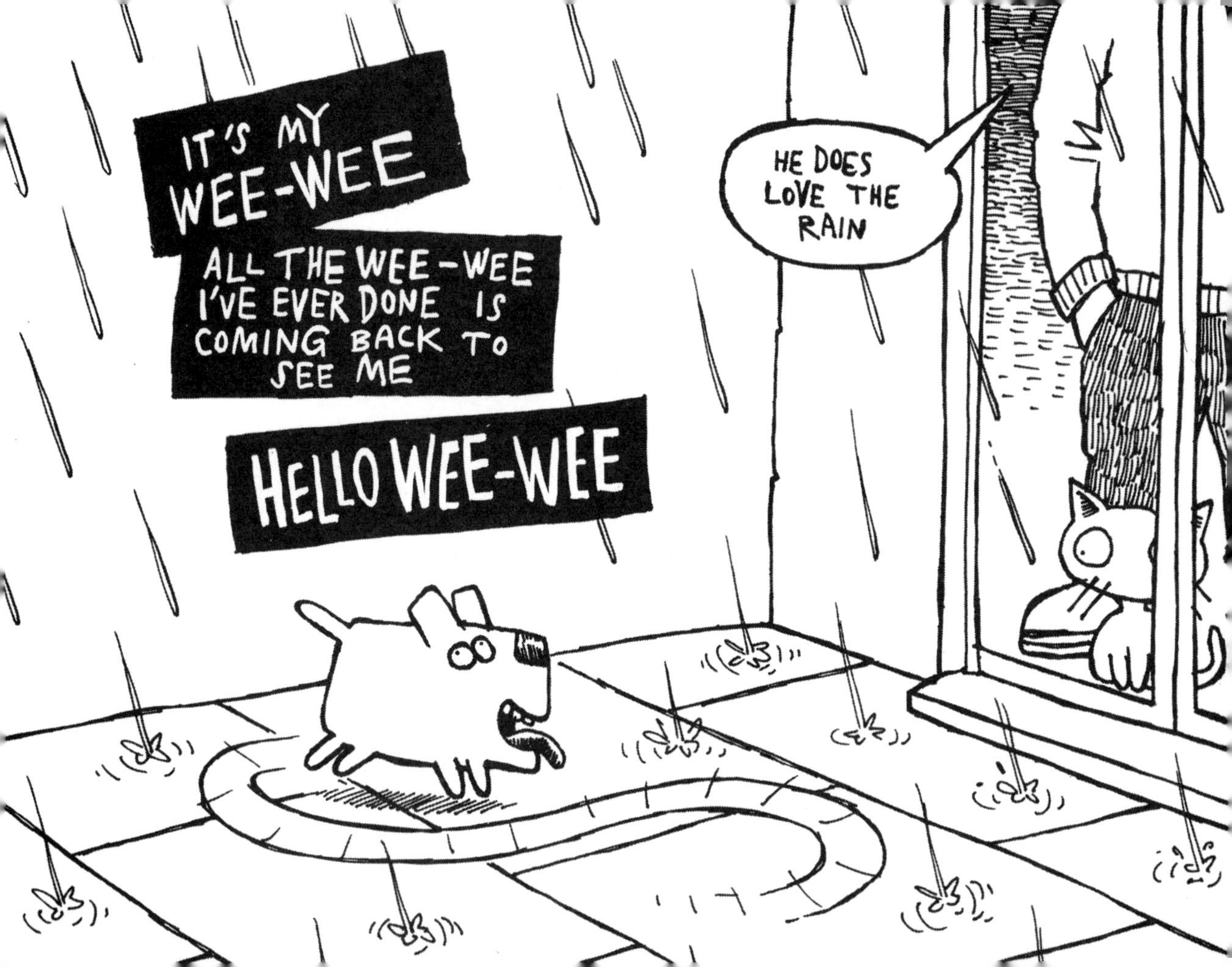
IT'S MY
WEE-WEE
ALL THE WEE-WEE
I'VE EVER DONE IS
COMING BACK TO
SEE ME
HELLO WEE-WEE
HE DOES
LOVE THE
RAIN

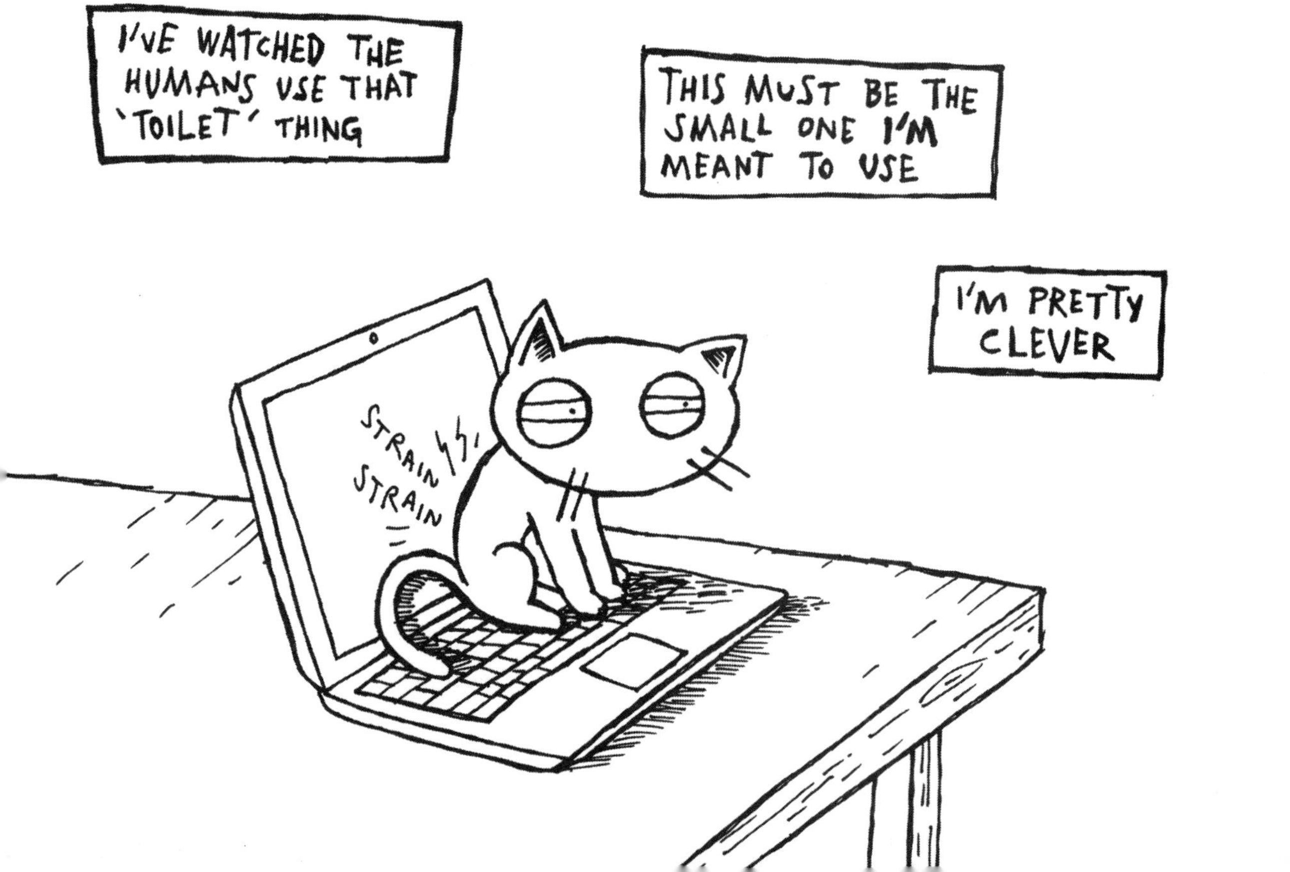
I'VE WATCHED THE HUMANS USE THAT 'TOILET' THING
THIS MUST BE THE SMALL ONE I'M MEANT TO USE
I'M PRETTY CLEVER
STRAIN
STRAIN

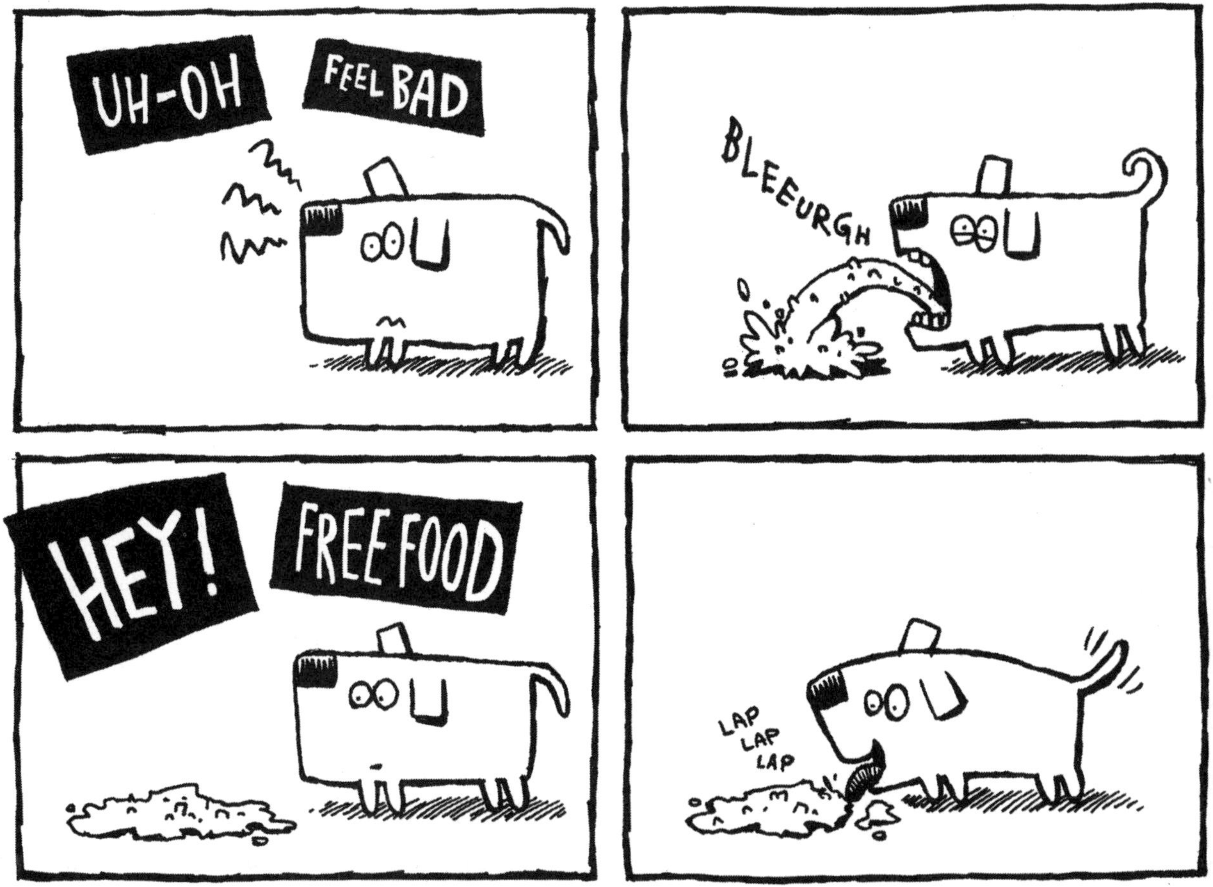
UH-OH
FEEL BAD
BLEEURGH
HEY!
FREE FOOD
LAP
LAP
LAP

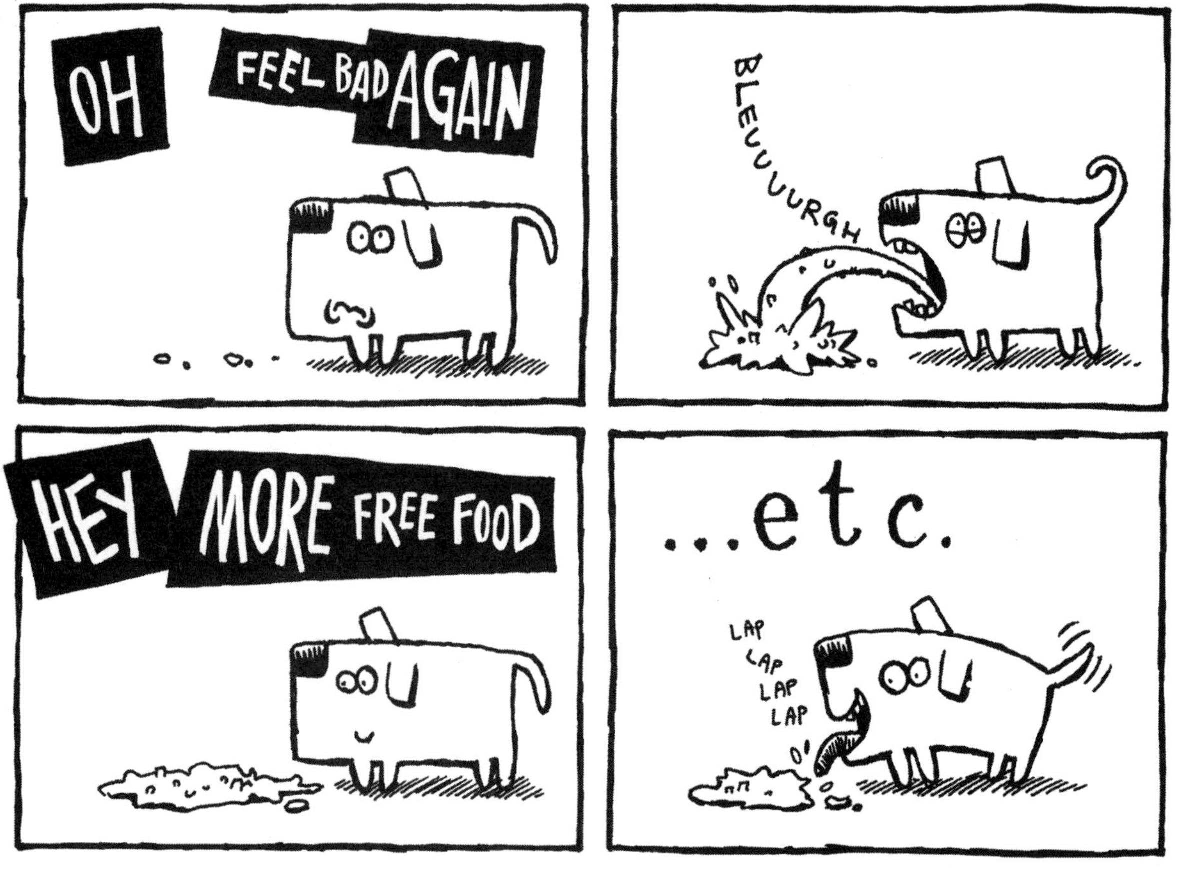
OH
FEEL BAD AGAIN
BLEUUUUURGH
HEY
MORE FREE FOOD
...etc.
LAP
LAP
LAP
LAP

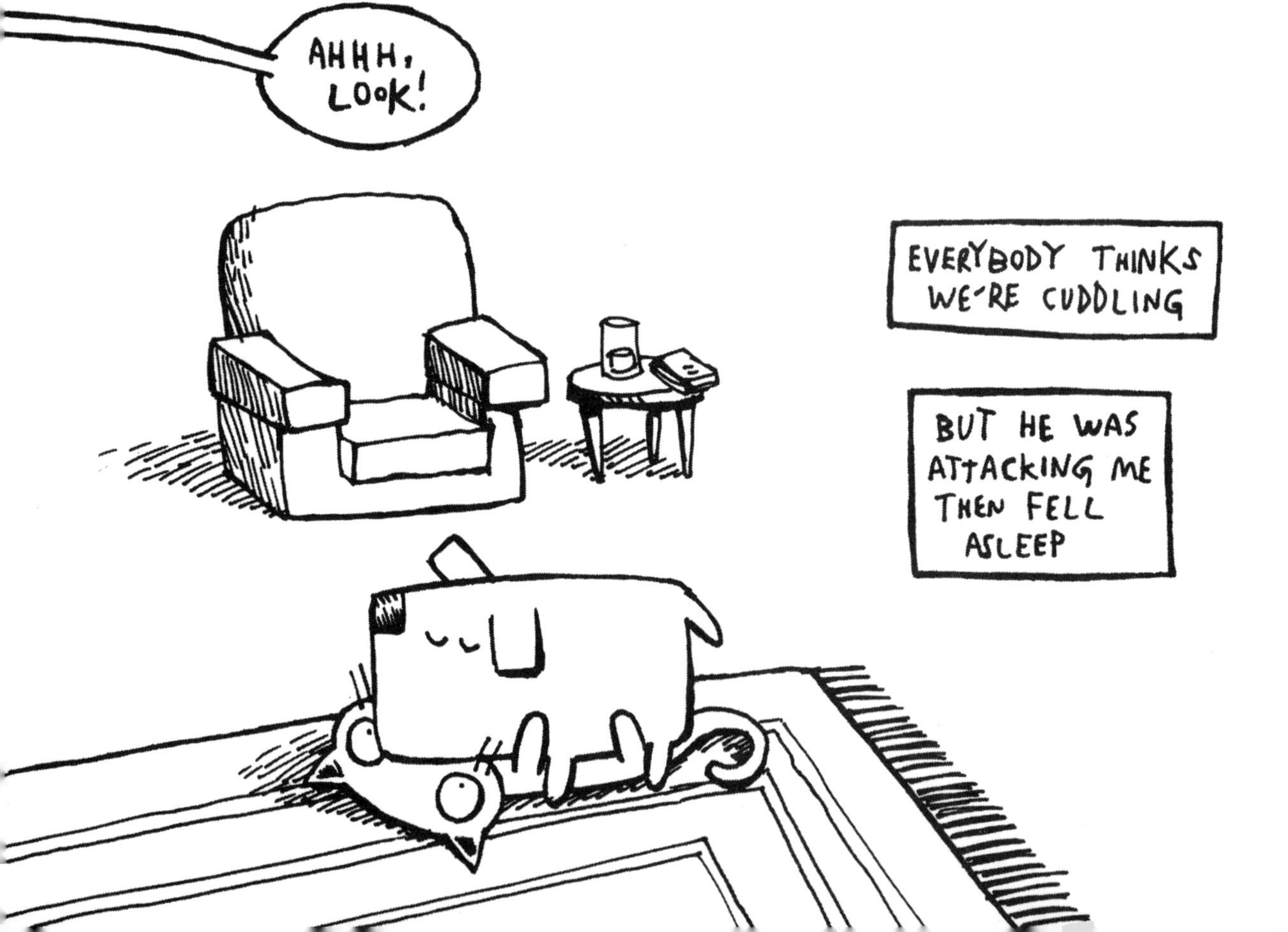
AHHH,
LOOK!
EVERYBODY THINKS WE'RE CUDDLING
BUT HE WAS ATTACKING ME THEN FELL ASLEEP

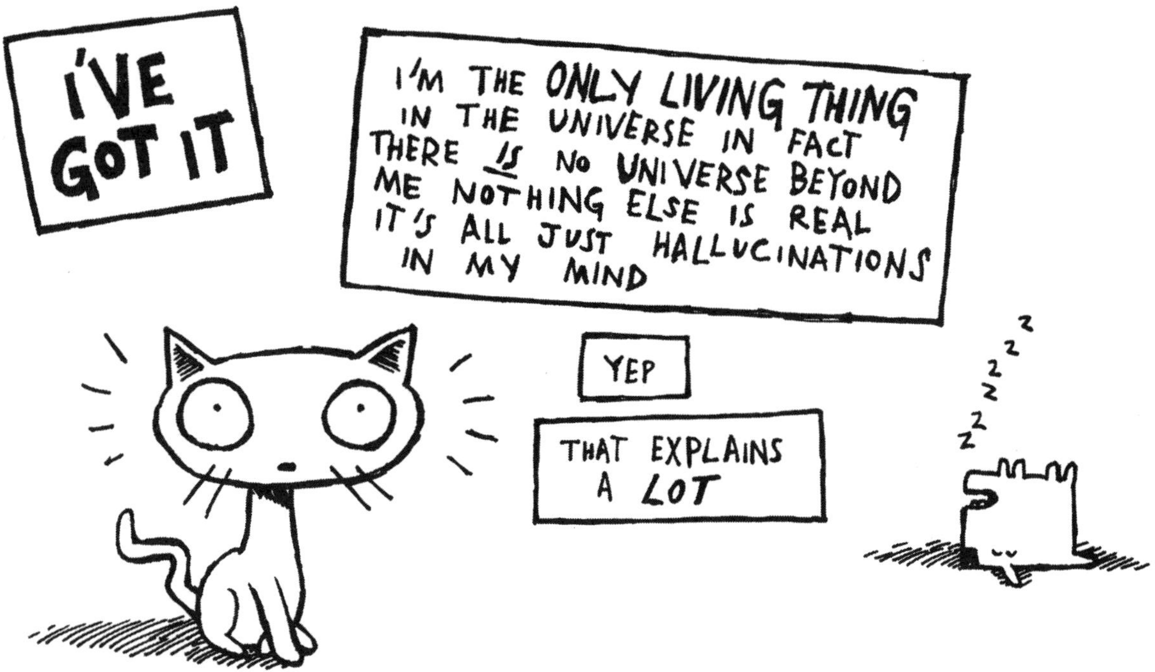
I'VE GOT IT
I'M THE ONLY LIVING THING IN THE UNIVERSE IN FACT THERE IS NO UNIVERSE BEYOND ME NOTHING ELSE IS REAL IT'S ALL JUST HALLUCINATIONS IN MY MIND
YEP
THAT EXPLAINS A LOT

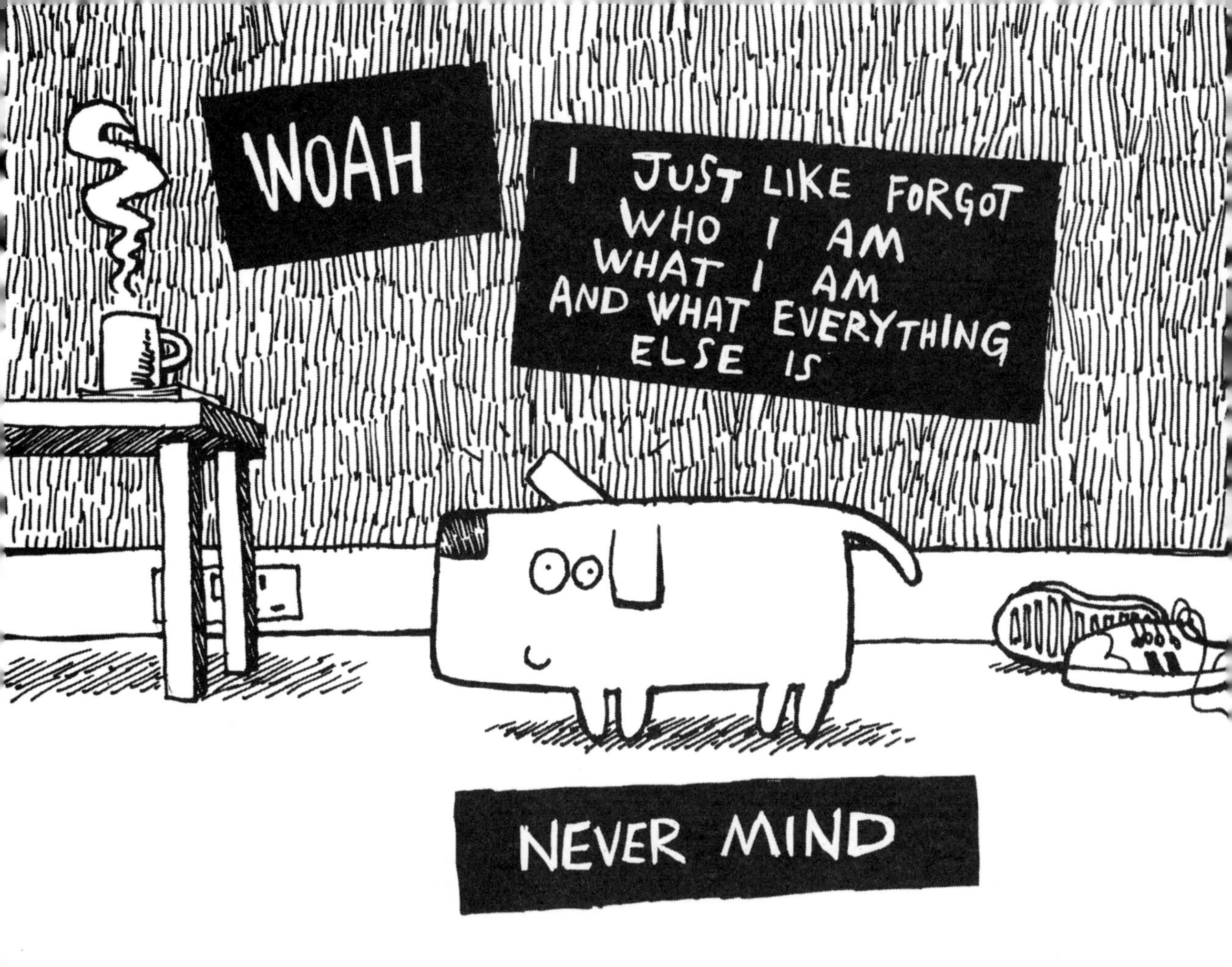
WOAH
I JUST LIKE FORGOT WHO I AM WHAT I AM AND WHAT EVERYTHING ELSE IS
NEVER MIND

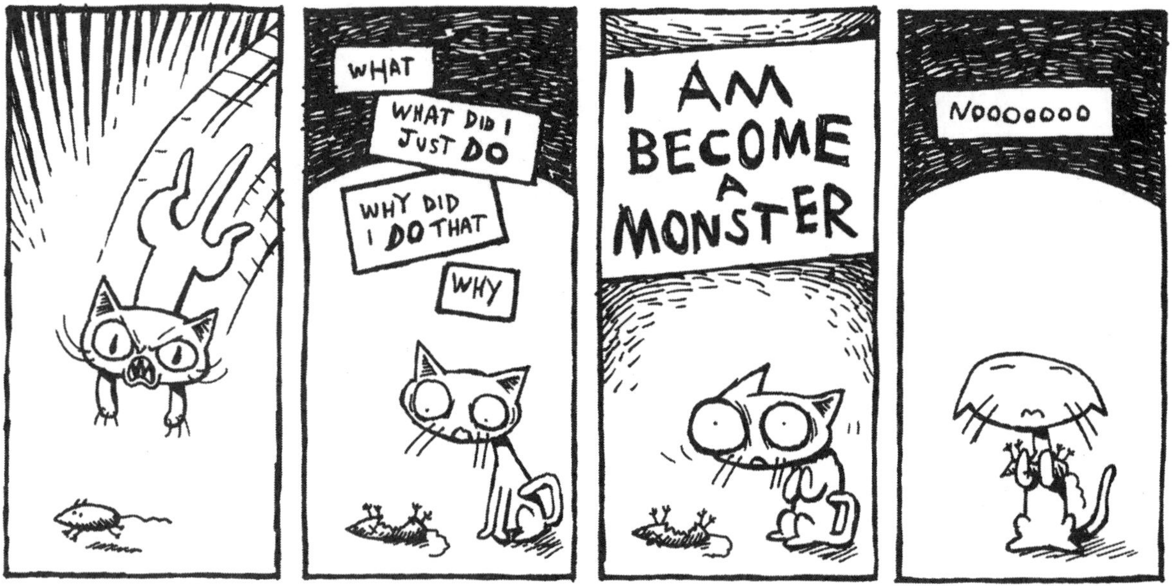
WHAT
WHAT DID I JUST DO
WHY DID I DO THAT
WHY
I AM BECOME A MONSTER
NOOOOOOO

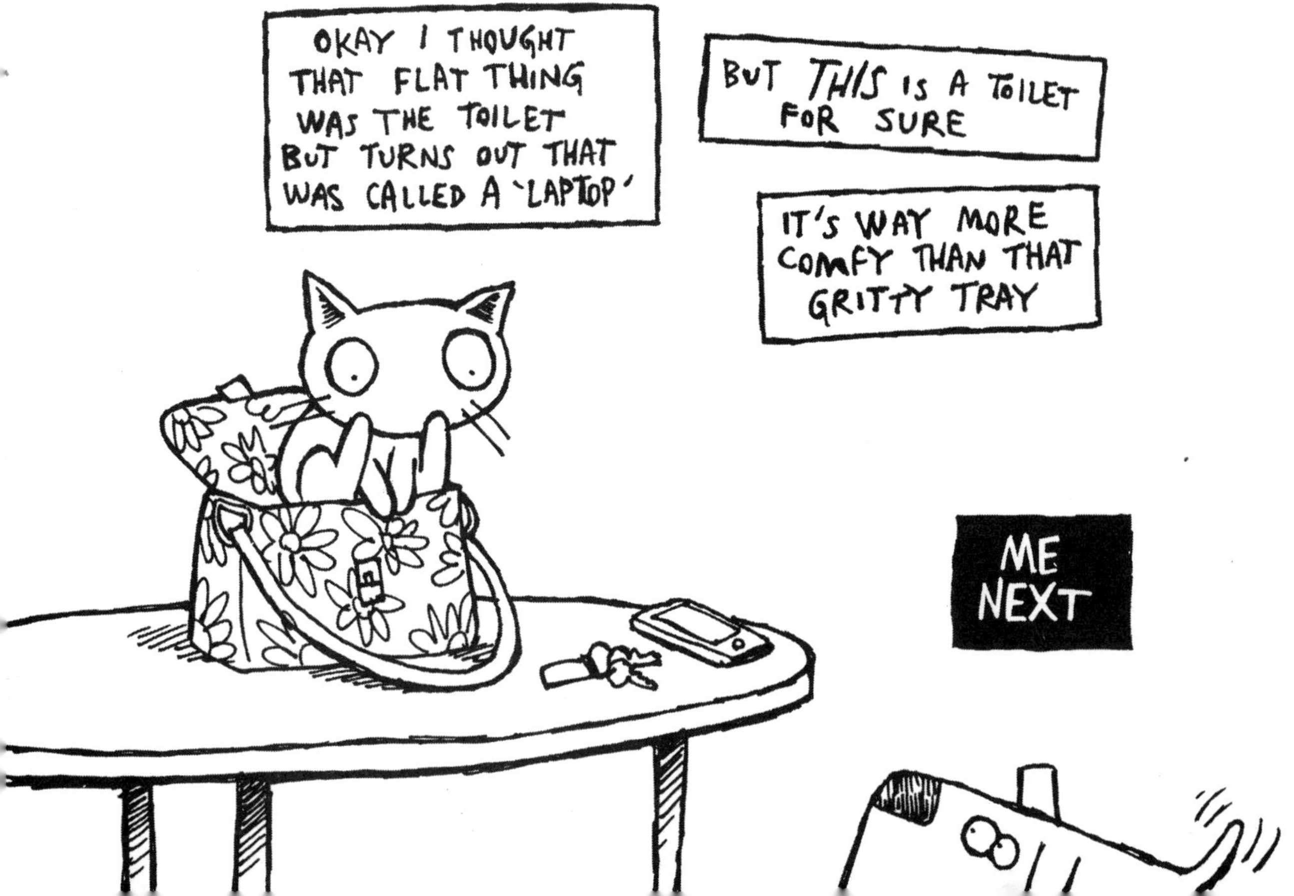
OKAY I THOUGHT THAT FLAT THING WAS THE TOILET BUT TURNS OUT THAT WAS CALLED A 'LAPTOP'
BUT *THIS* IS A TOILET FOR SURE
IT'S WAY MORE COMFY THAN THAT GRITTY TRAY
ME NEXT

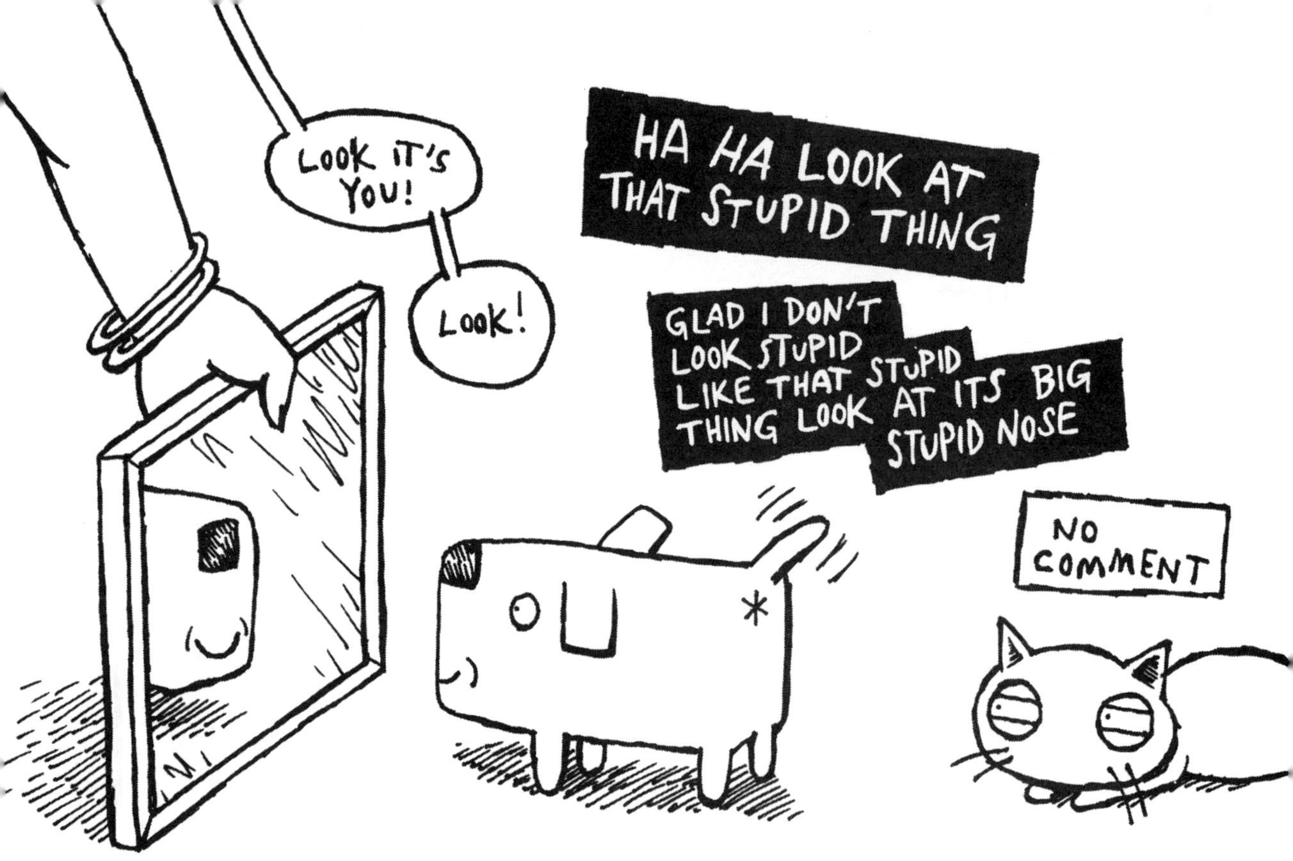
LOOK IT'S YOU!
LOOK!
HA HA LOOK AT THAT STUPID THING
GLAD I DON'T LOOK STUPID LIKE THAT STUPID THING LOOK AT ITS BIG STUPID NOSE
NO COMMENT

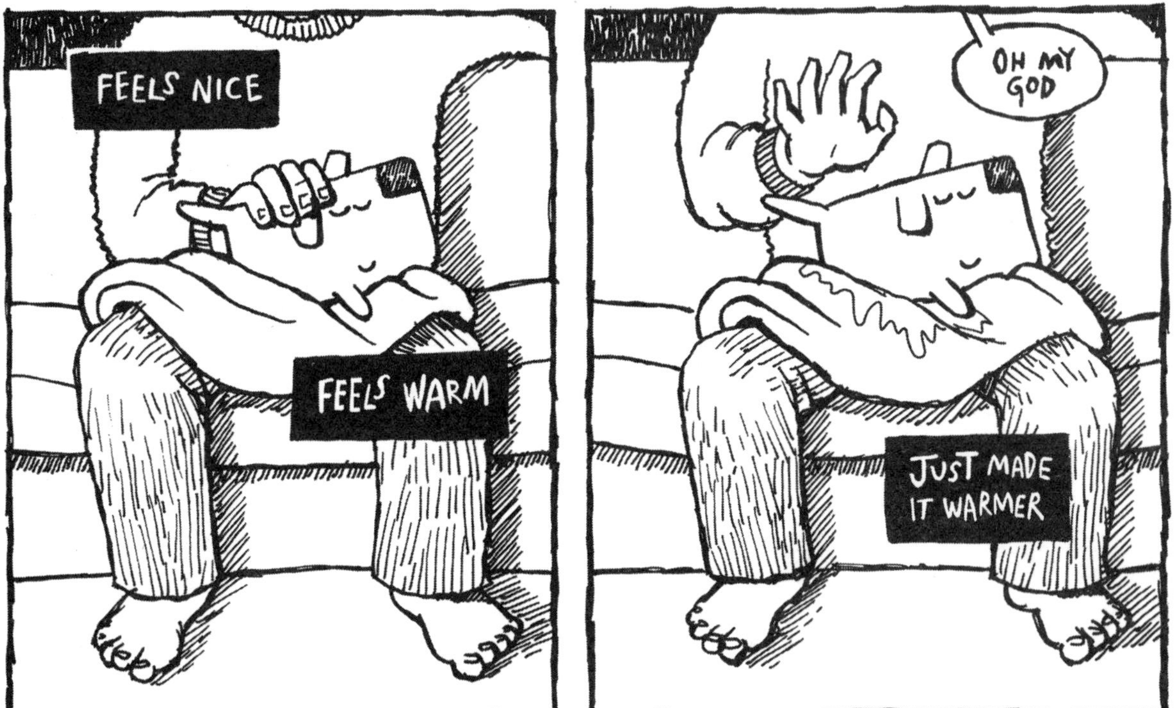
FEELS NICE
FEELS WARM
OH MY GOD
JUST MADE IT WARMER

I WONDER WHAT HE'S THINKING ABOUT

[BUFFERING]

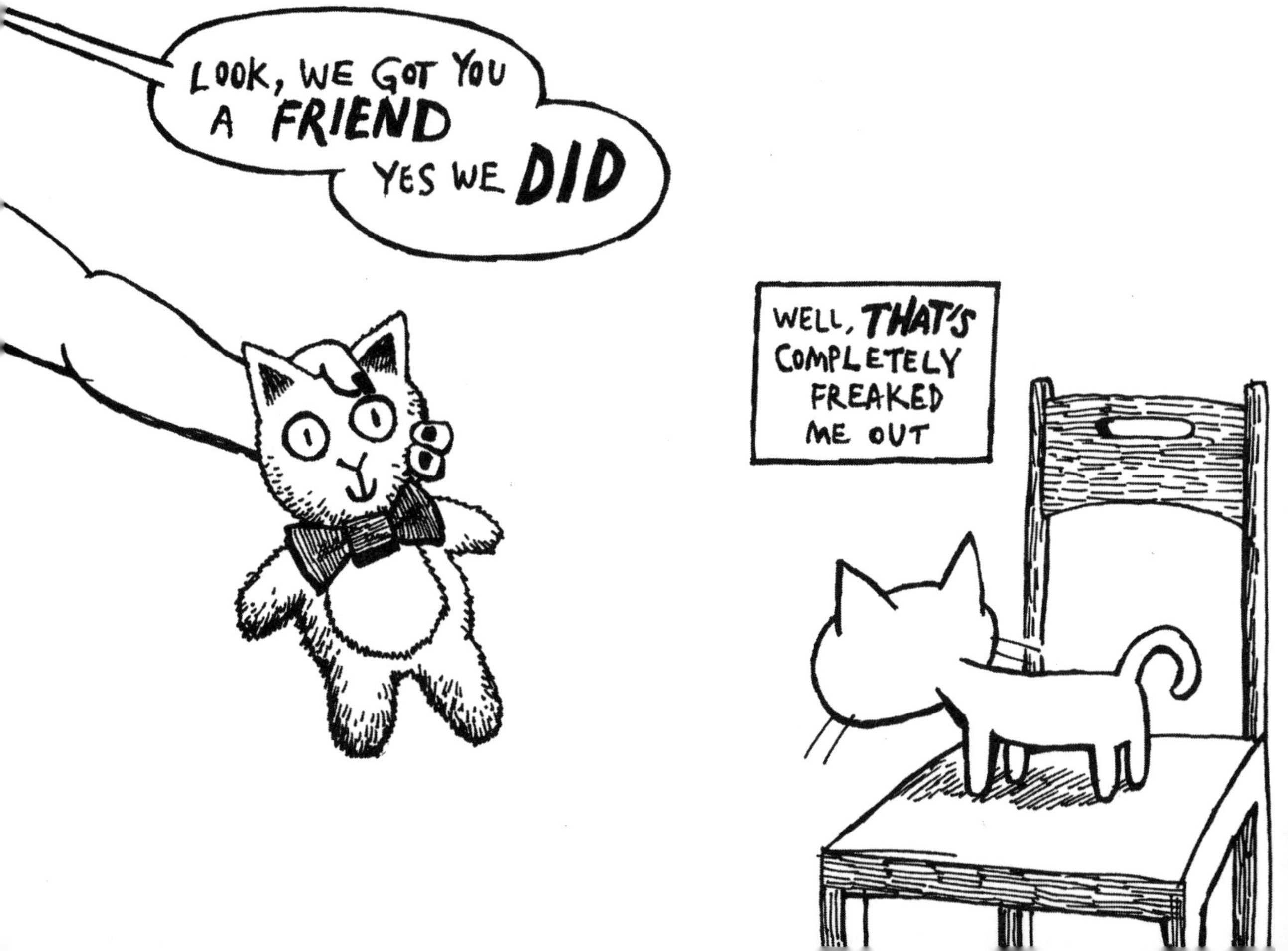

LOOK, WE GOT YOU A FRIEND YES WE DID
WELL, THAT'S COMPLETELY FREAKED ME OUT

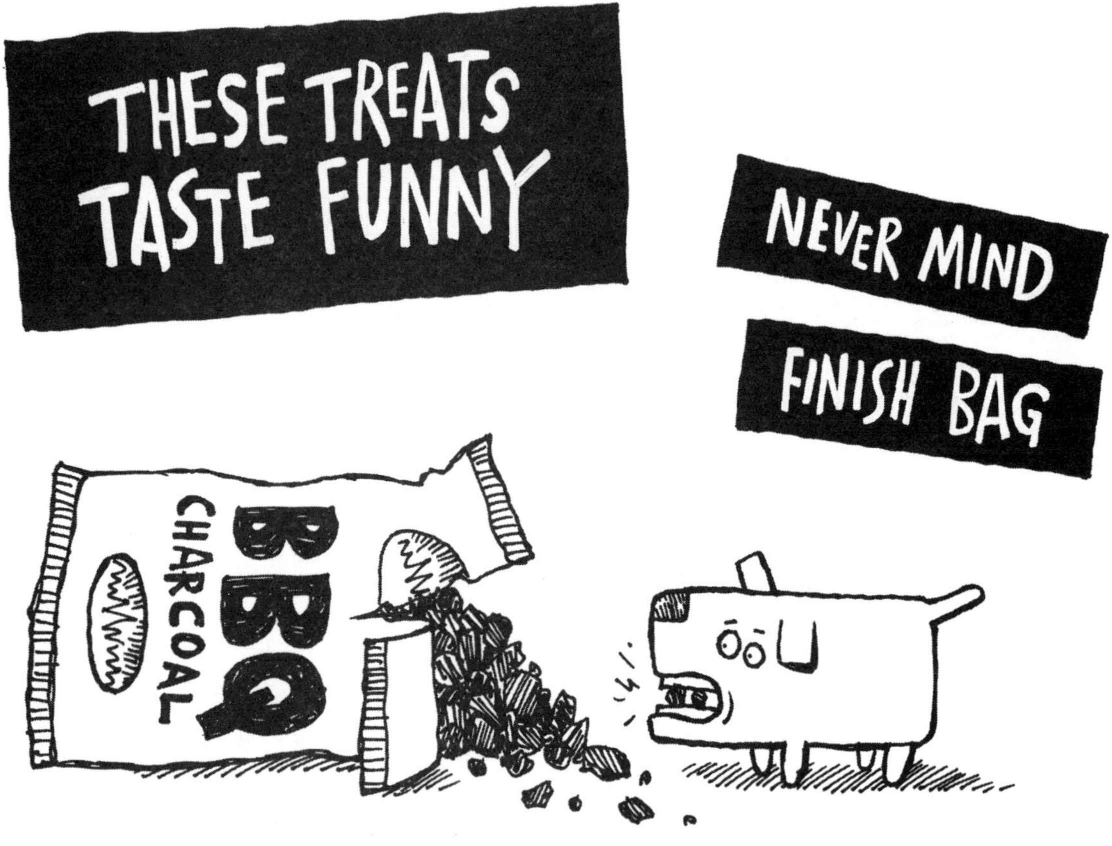
THESE TREATS TASTE FUNNY
NEVER MIND
FINISH BAG
BBQ
CHARCOAL

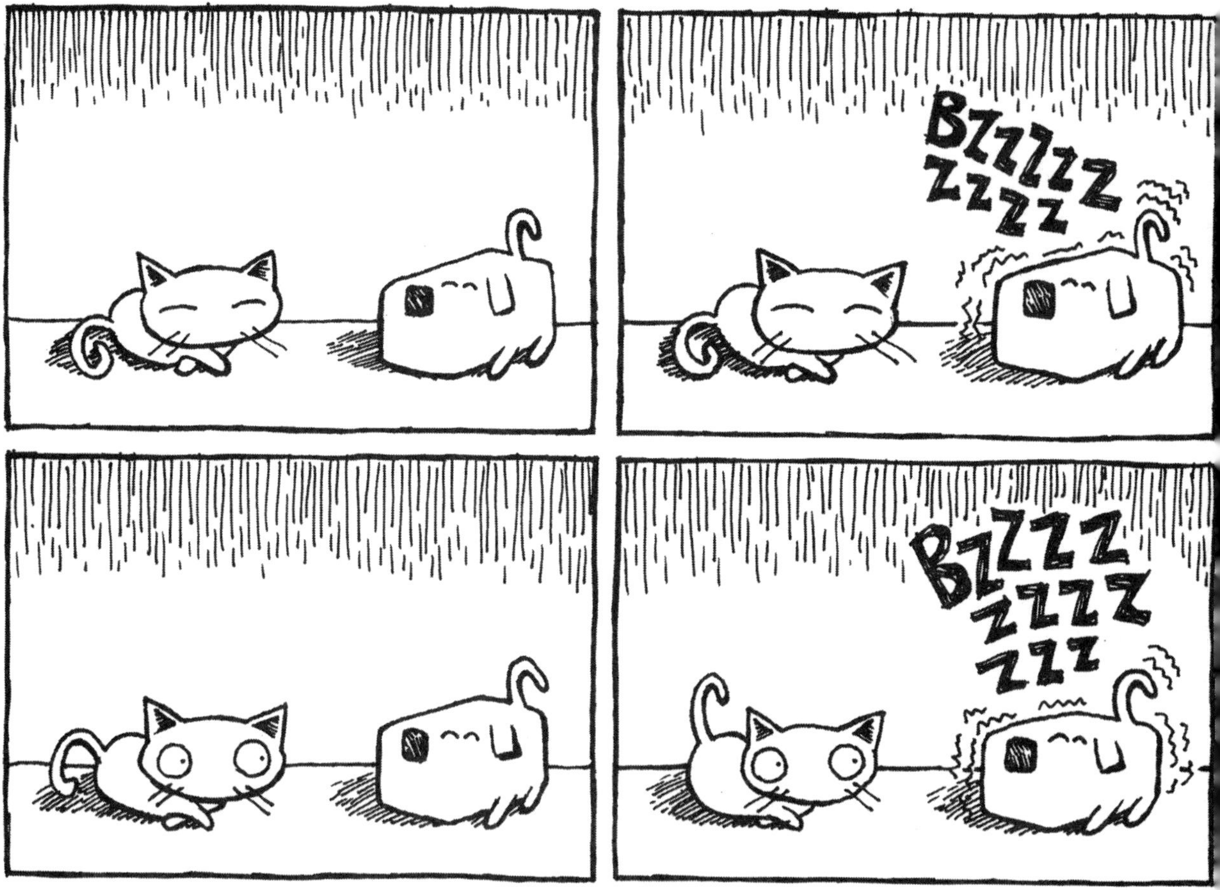
BZZZZZ
ZZZZ
BZZZZ
ZZZZ
ZZZ

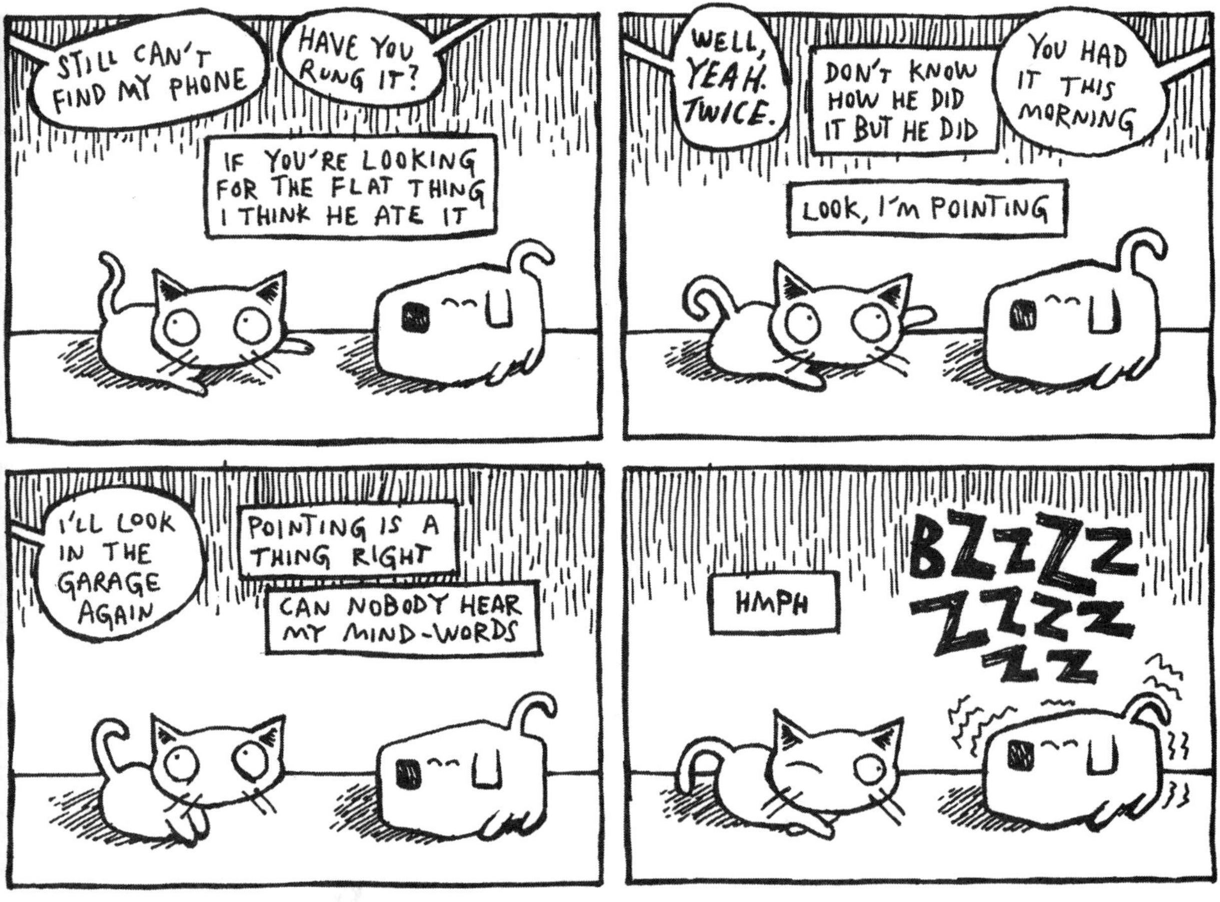
STILL CAN'T FIND MY PHONE
HAVE YOU RUNG IT?
IF YOU'RE LOOKING FOR THE FLAT THING I THINK HE ATE IT
WELL, YEAH. TWICE.
DON'T KNOW HOW HE DID IT BUT HE DID
YOU HAD IT THIS MORNING
LOOK, I'M POINTING
I'LL LOOK IN THE GARAGE AGAIN
POINTING IS A THING RIGHT
CAN NOBODY HEAR MY MIND-WORDS
HMPH
BZZZZ ZZZZ ZZ

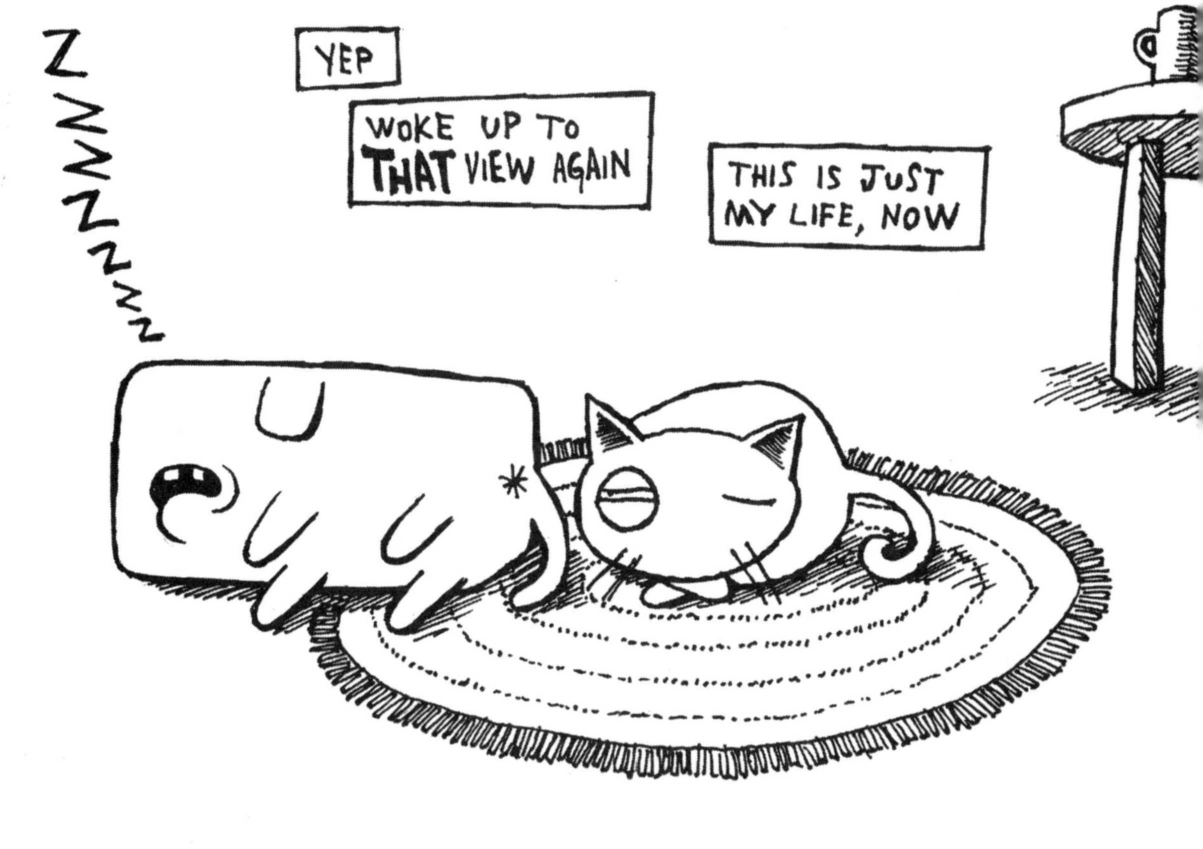
ZZZZZzzzz
YEP
WOKE UP TO THAT VIEW AGAIN
THIS IS JUST MY LIFE, NOW

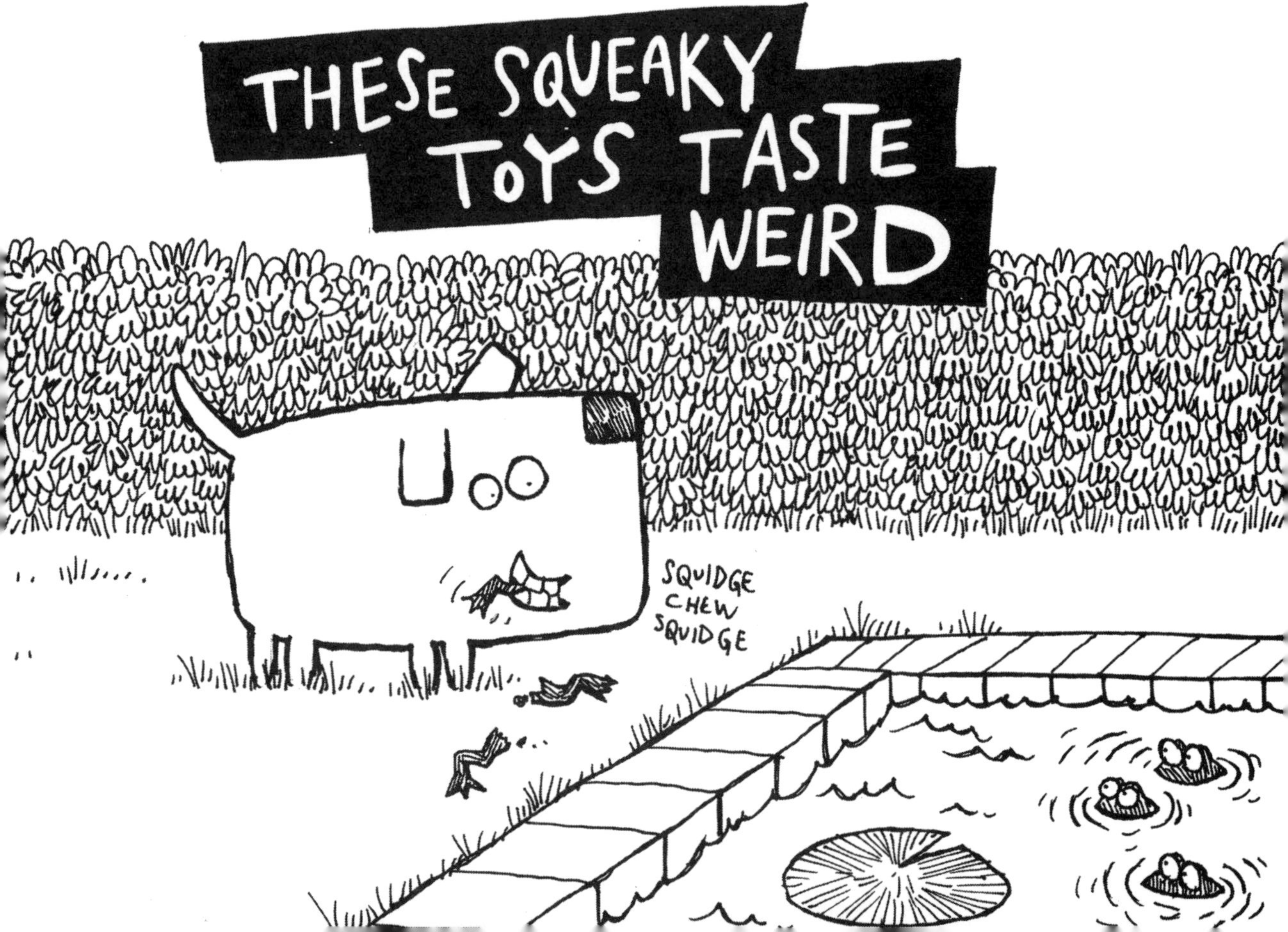
THESE SQUEAKY TOYS TASTE WEIRD
SQUIDGE
CHEW
SQUIDGE

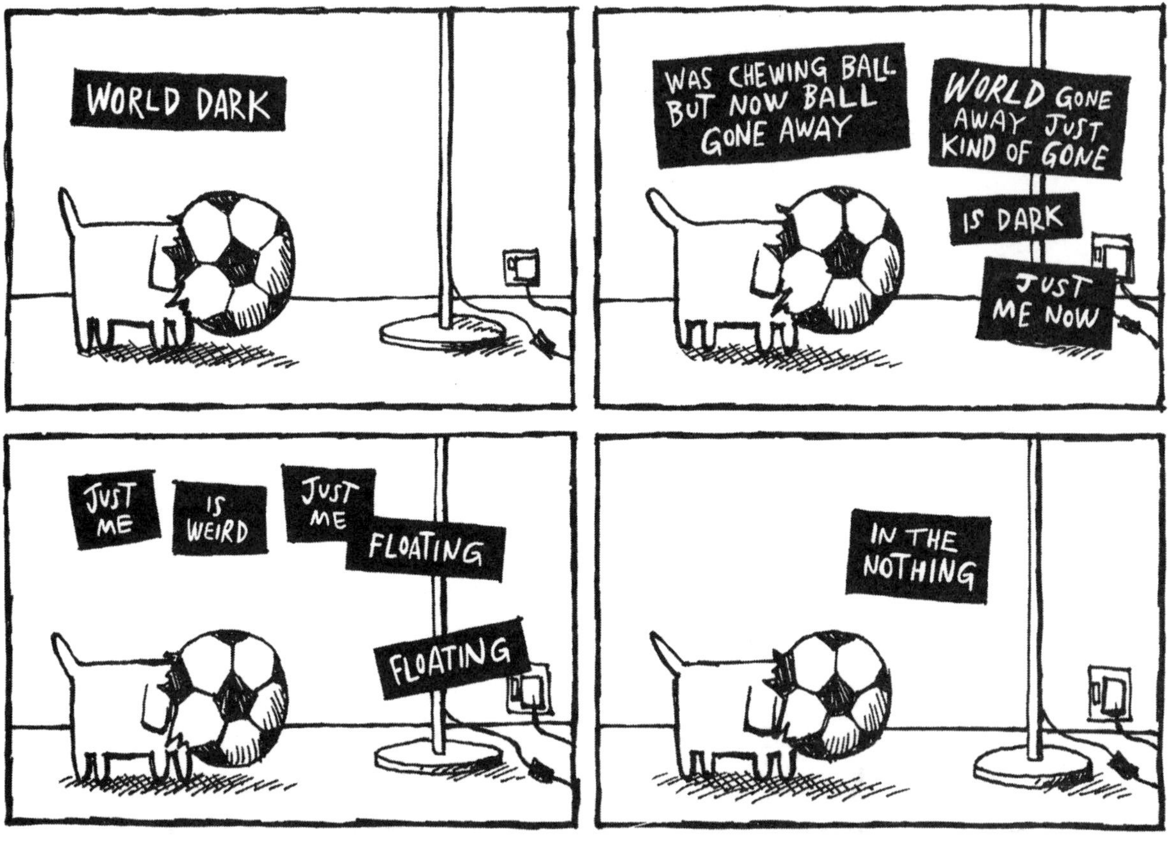
WORLD DARK
WAS CHEWING BALL BUT NOW BALL GONE AWAY
WORLD GONE AWAY JUST KIND OF GONE
IS DARK
JUST ME NOW
JUST ME
IS WEIRD
JUST ME
FLOATING
FLOATING
IN THE NOTHING

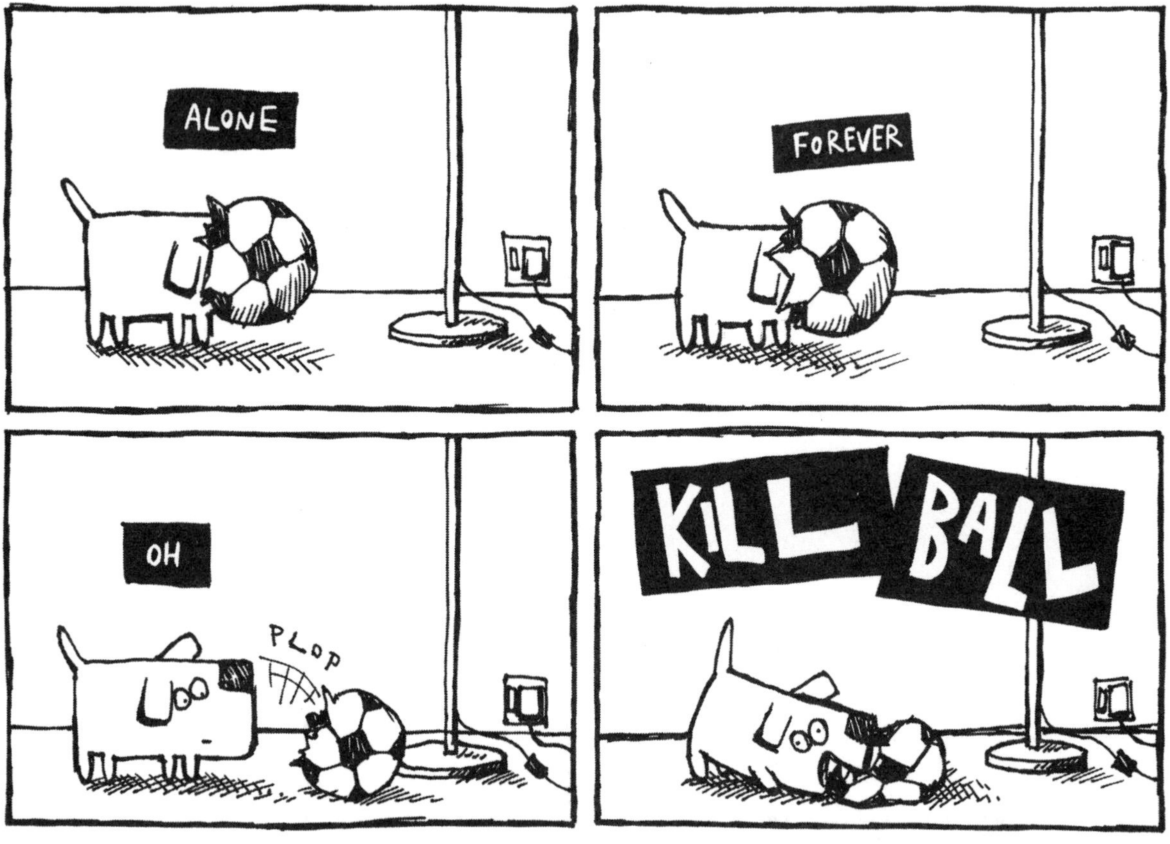
ALONE
FOREVER
OH
PLOP
KILL
BALL

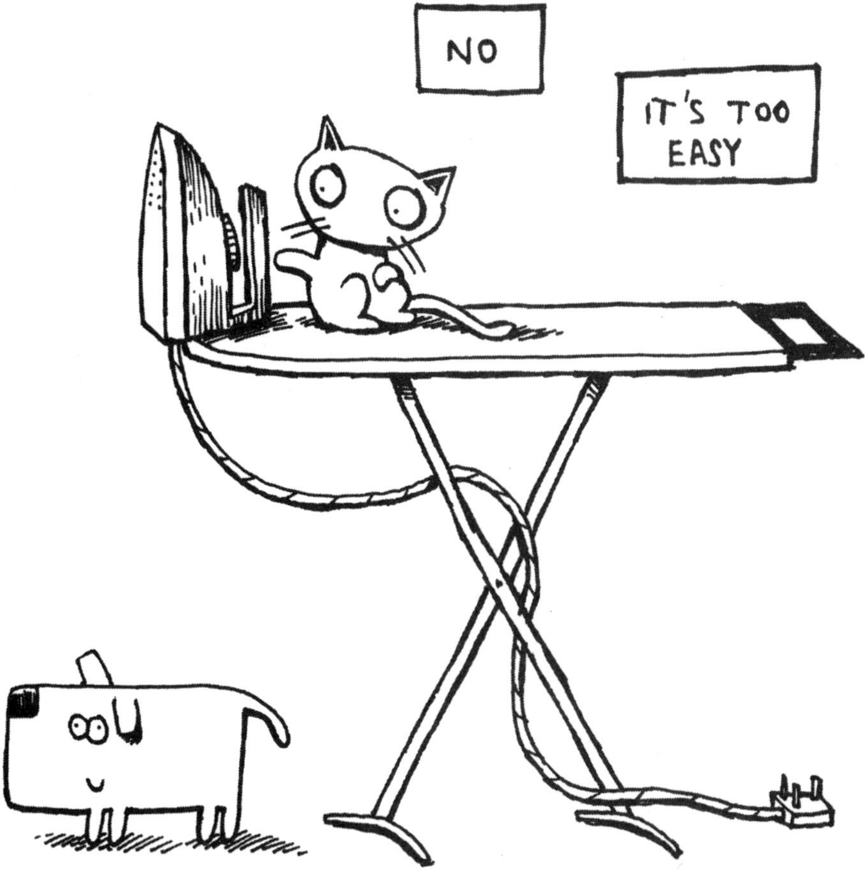
NO
IT'S TOO EASY

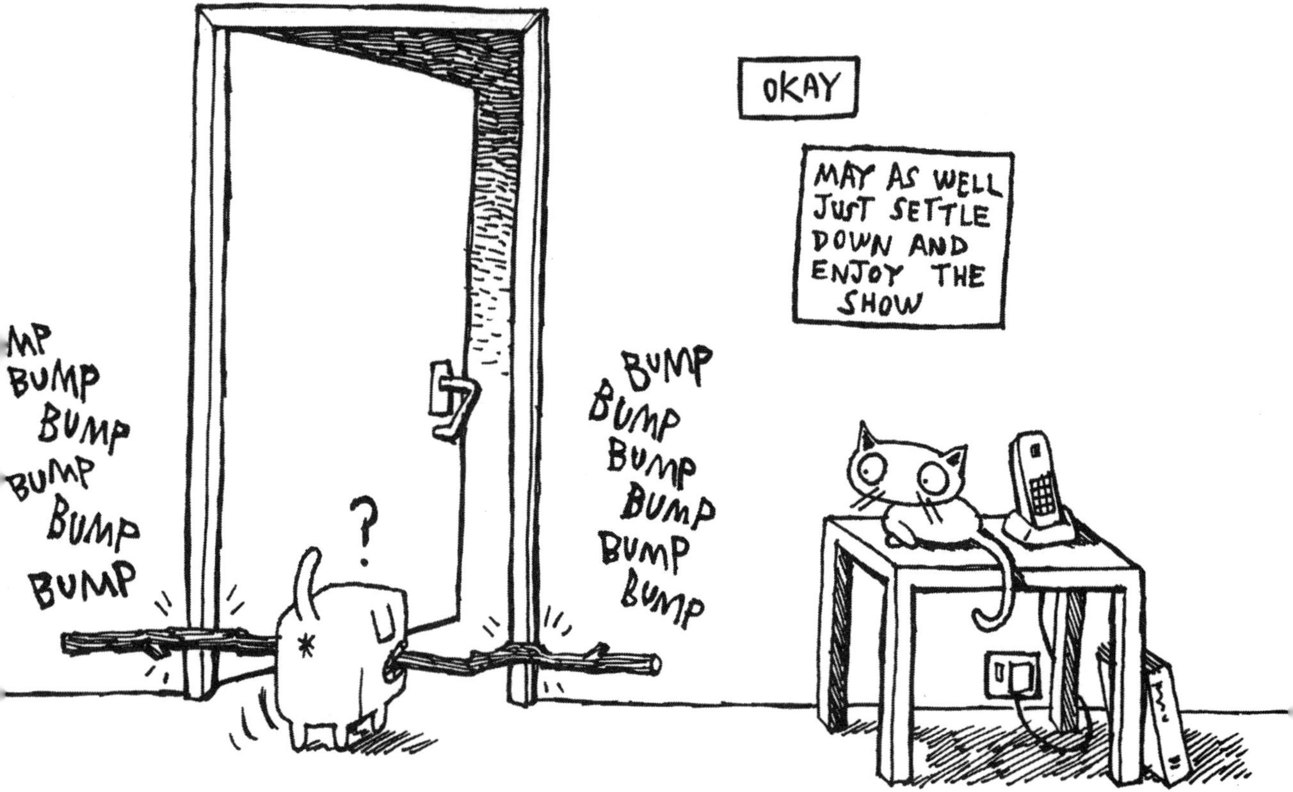
MP
BUMP
BUMP
BUMP
BUMP
BUMP
?
BUMP
BUMP
BUMP
BUMP
BUMP
BUMP
OKAY
MAY AS WELL JUST SETTLE DOWN AND ENJOY THE SHOW

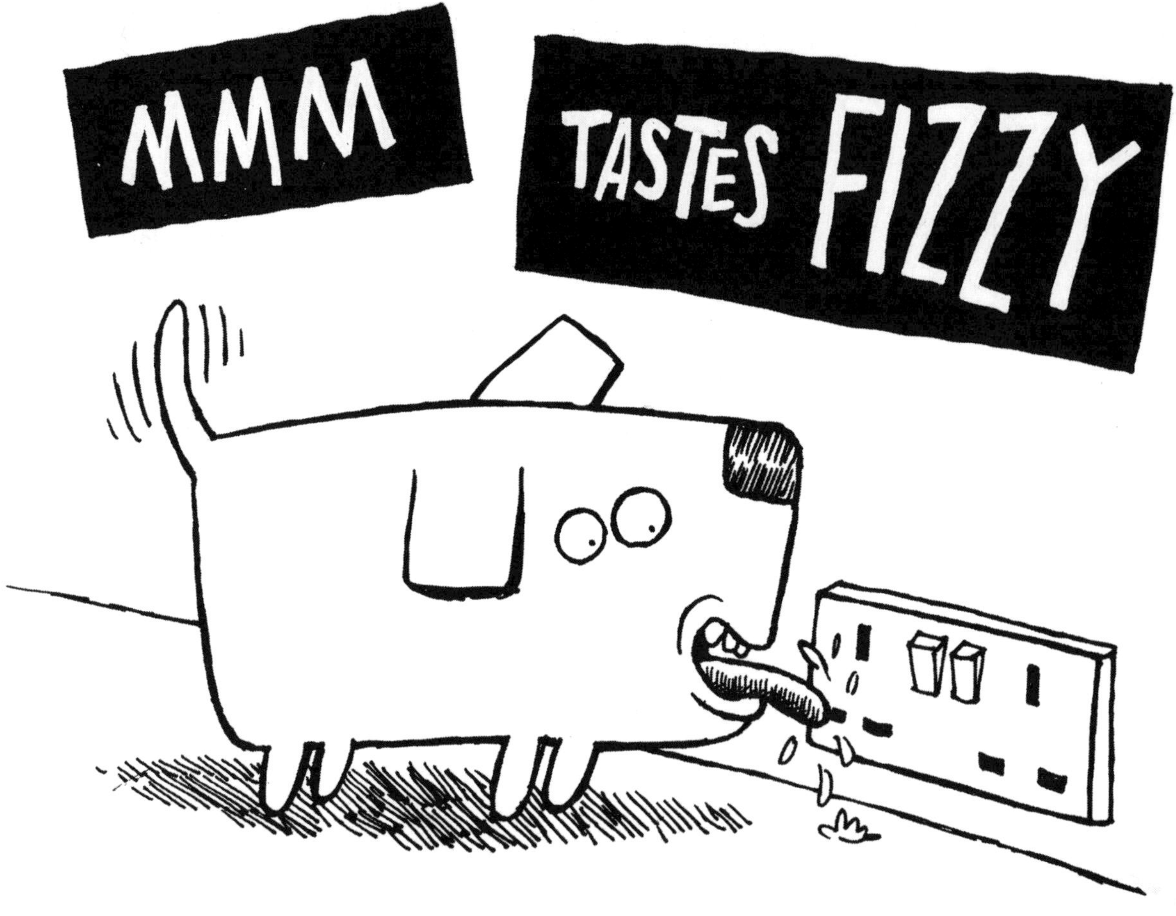
MMM
TASTES FIZZY

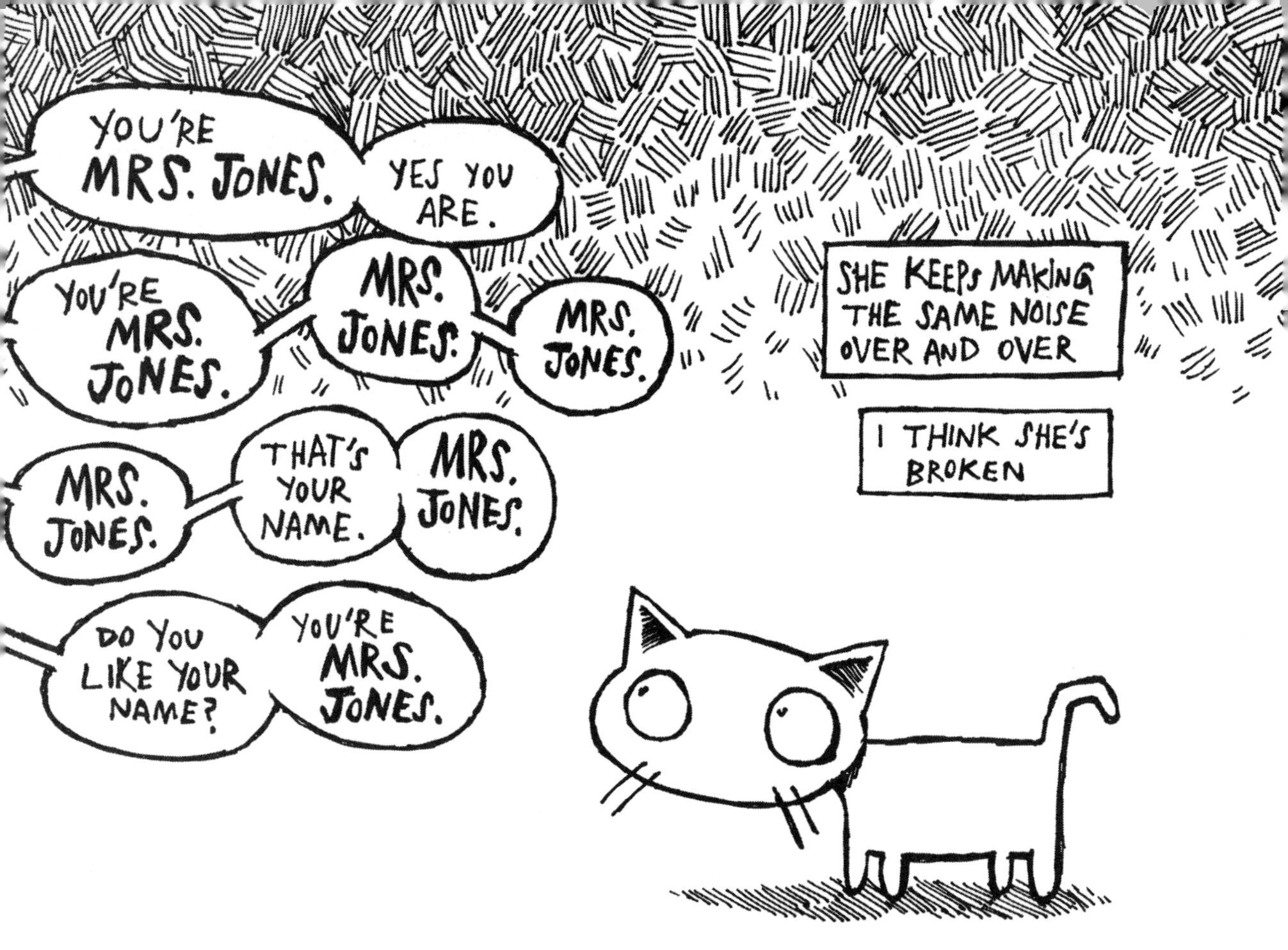
YOU'RE MRS. JONES.
YES YOU ARE.
YOU'RE MRS. JONES.
MRS. JONES.
MRS. JONES.
MRS. JONES.
THAT'S YOUR NAME.
MRS. JONES.
DO YOU LIKE YOUR NAME?
YOU'RE MRS. JONES.
SHE KEEPS MAKING THE SAME NOISE OVER AND OVER
I THINK SHE'S BROKEN

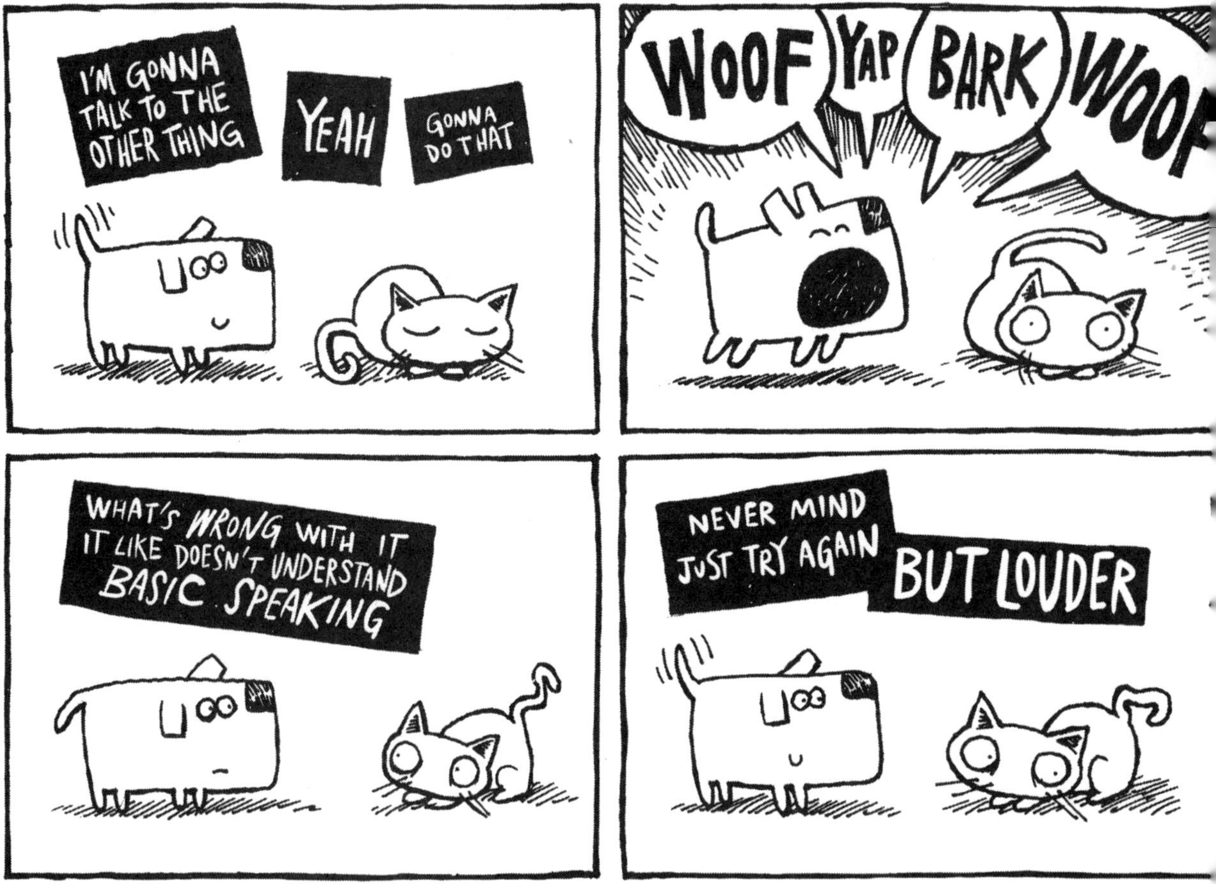
I'M GONNA TALK TO THE OTHER THING
YEAH
GONNA DO THAT
WOOF
YAP
BARK
WOOF
WHAT'S WRONG WITH IT IT LIKE DOESN'T UNDERSTAND BASIC SPEAKING
NEVER MIND JUST TRY AGAIN
BUT LOUDER

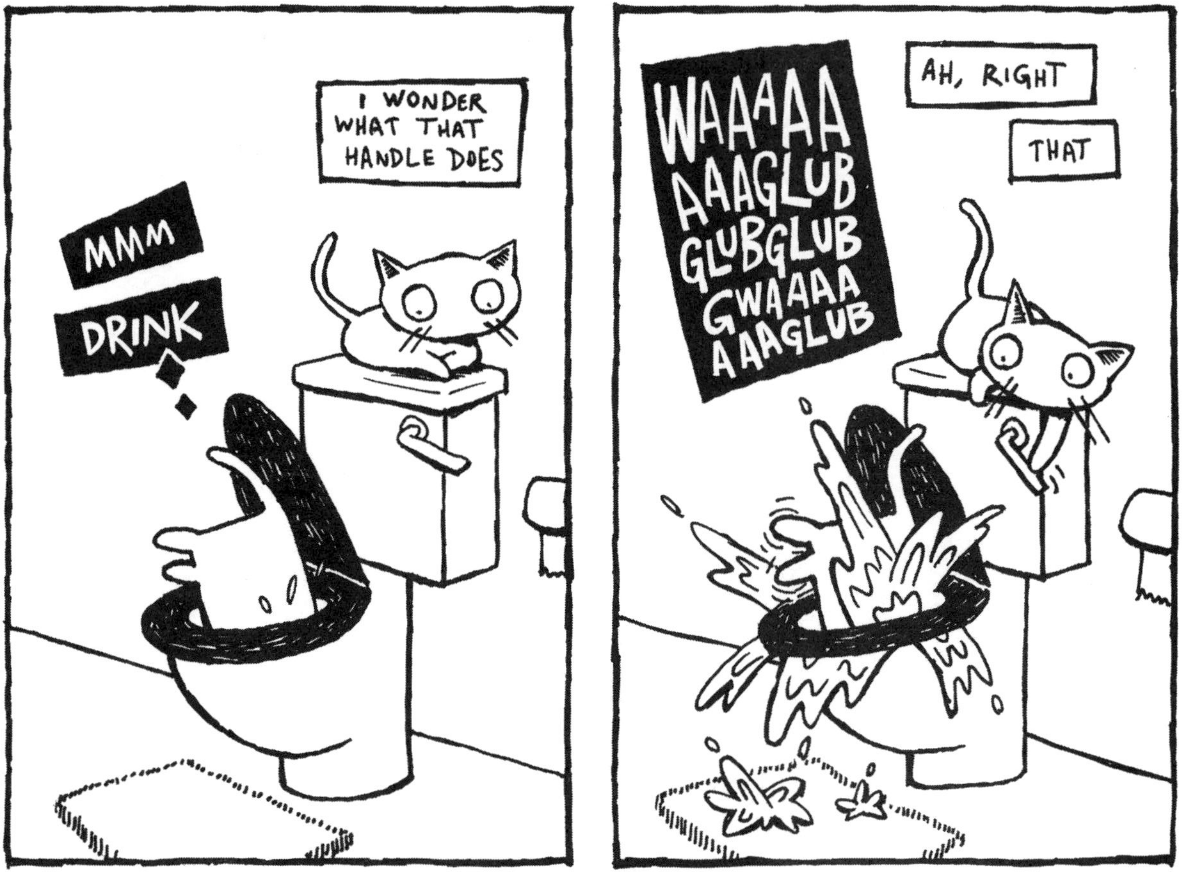
I WONDER WHAT THAT HANDLE DOES
MMM
DRINK
WAAAAA AAAGLUB GLUBGLUB GWAAAA AAAGLUB
AH, RIGHT
THAT

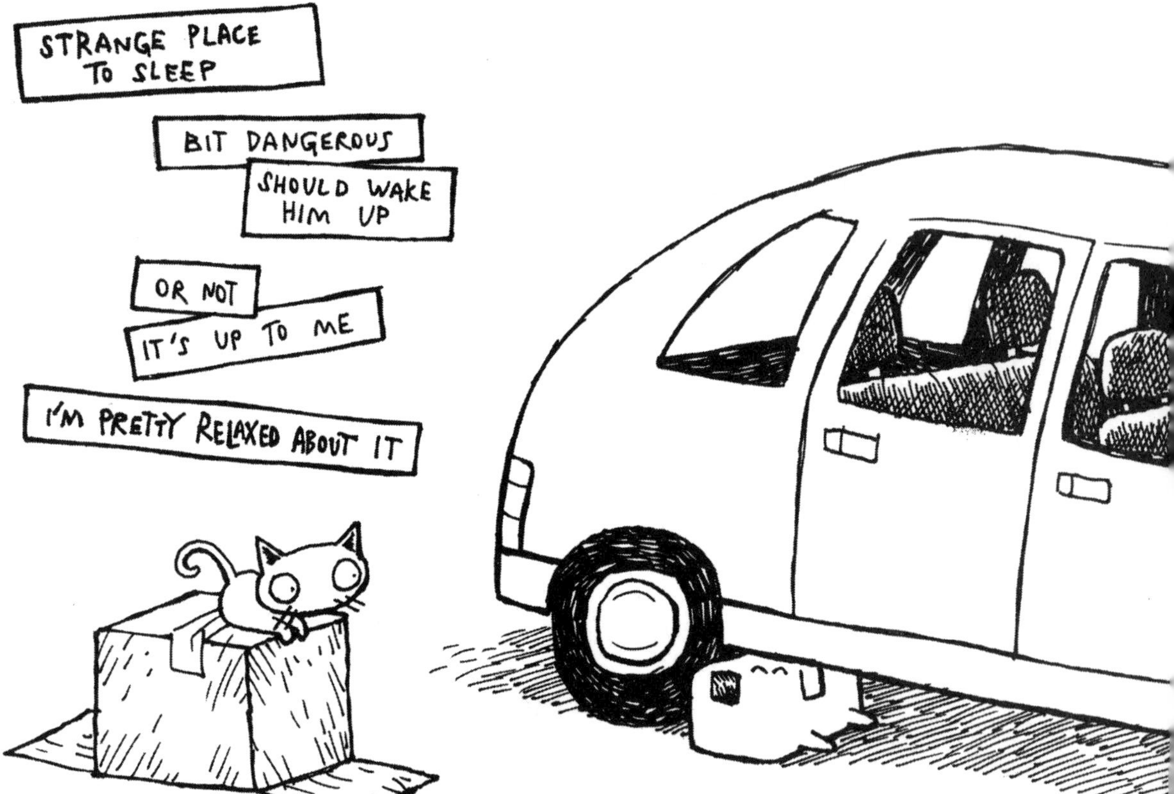
STRANGE PLACE TO SLEEP
BIT DANGEROUS
SHOULD WAKE HIM UP
OR NOT
IT'S UP TO ME
I'M PRETTY RELAXED ABOUT IT

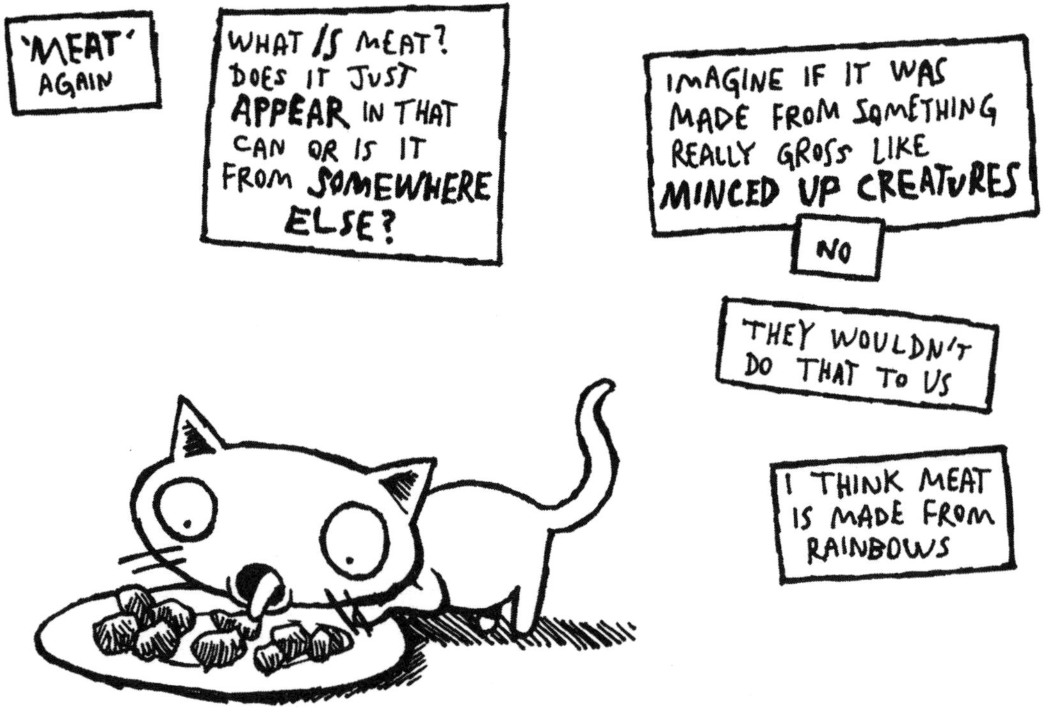
'MEAT' AGAIN
WHAT IS MEAT? DOES IT JUST APPEAR IN THAT CAN OR IS IT FROM SOMEWHERE ELSE?
IMAGINE IF IT WAS MADE FROM SOMETHING REALLY GROSS LIKE MINCED UP CREATURES
NO
THEY WOULDN'T DO THAT TO US
I THINK MEAT IS MADE FROM RAINBOWS

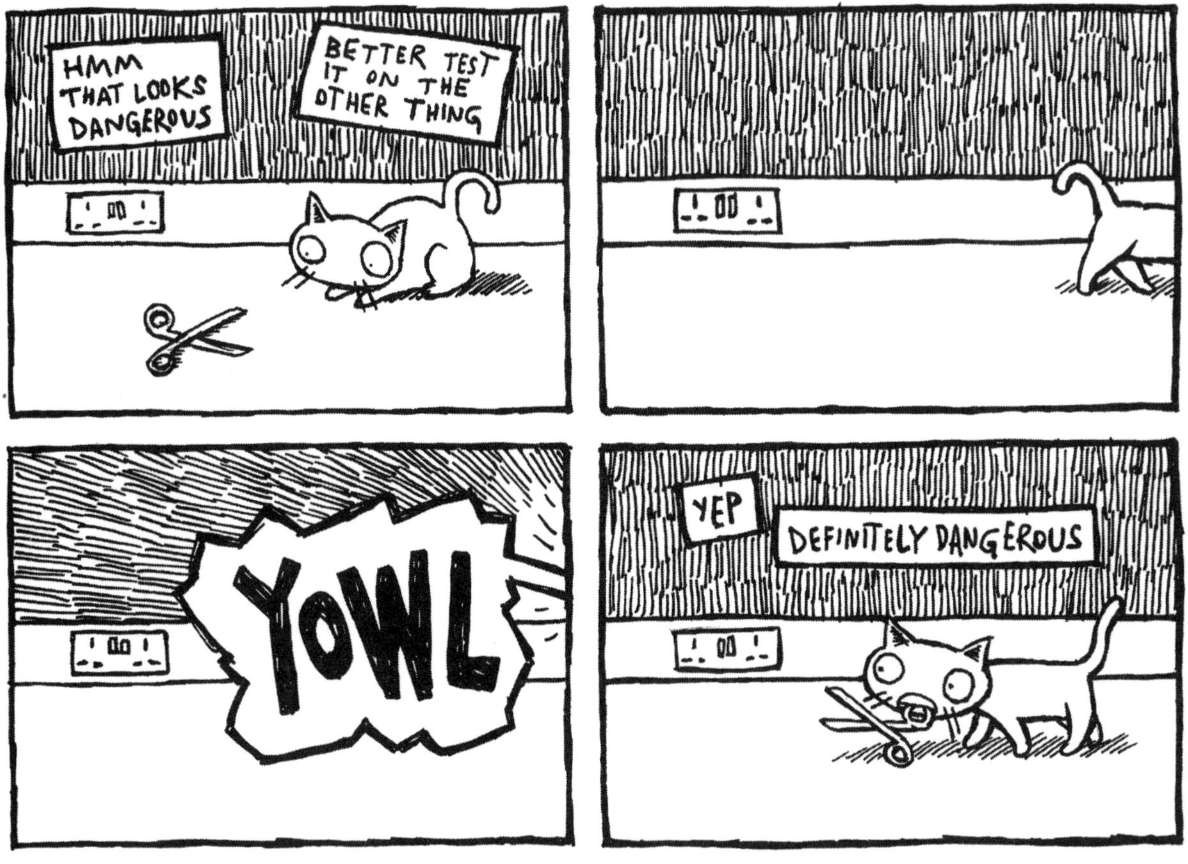
HMM
THAT LOOKS
DANGEROUS
BETTER TEST
IT ON THE
OTHER THING
YOWL
YEP
DEFINITELY DANGEROUS

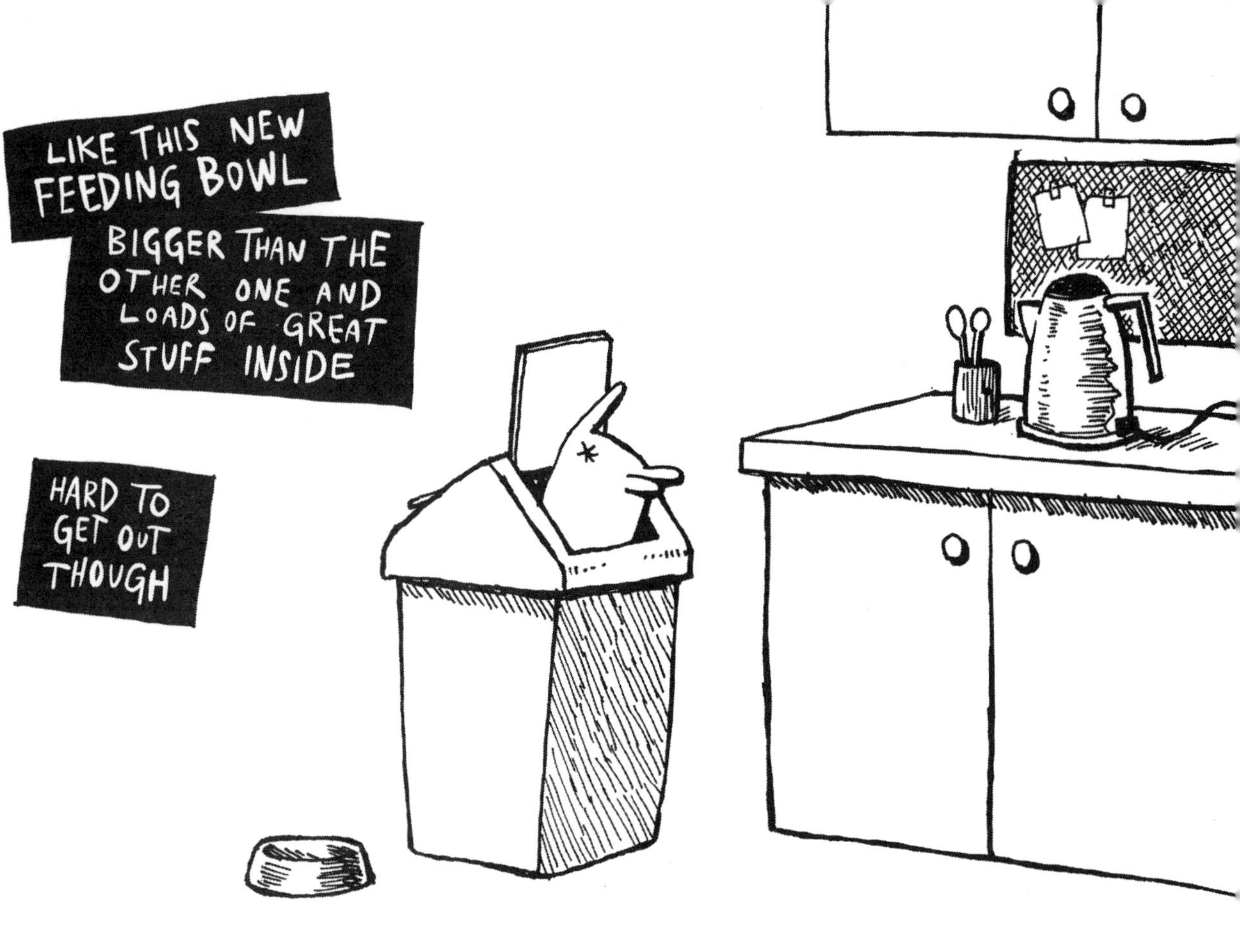
LIKE THIS NEW FEEDING BOWL
BIGGER THAN THE OTHER ONE AND LOADS OF GREAT STUFF INSIDE
HARD TO GET OUT THOUGH

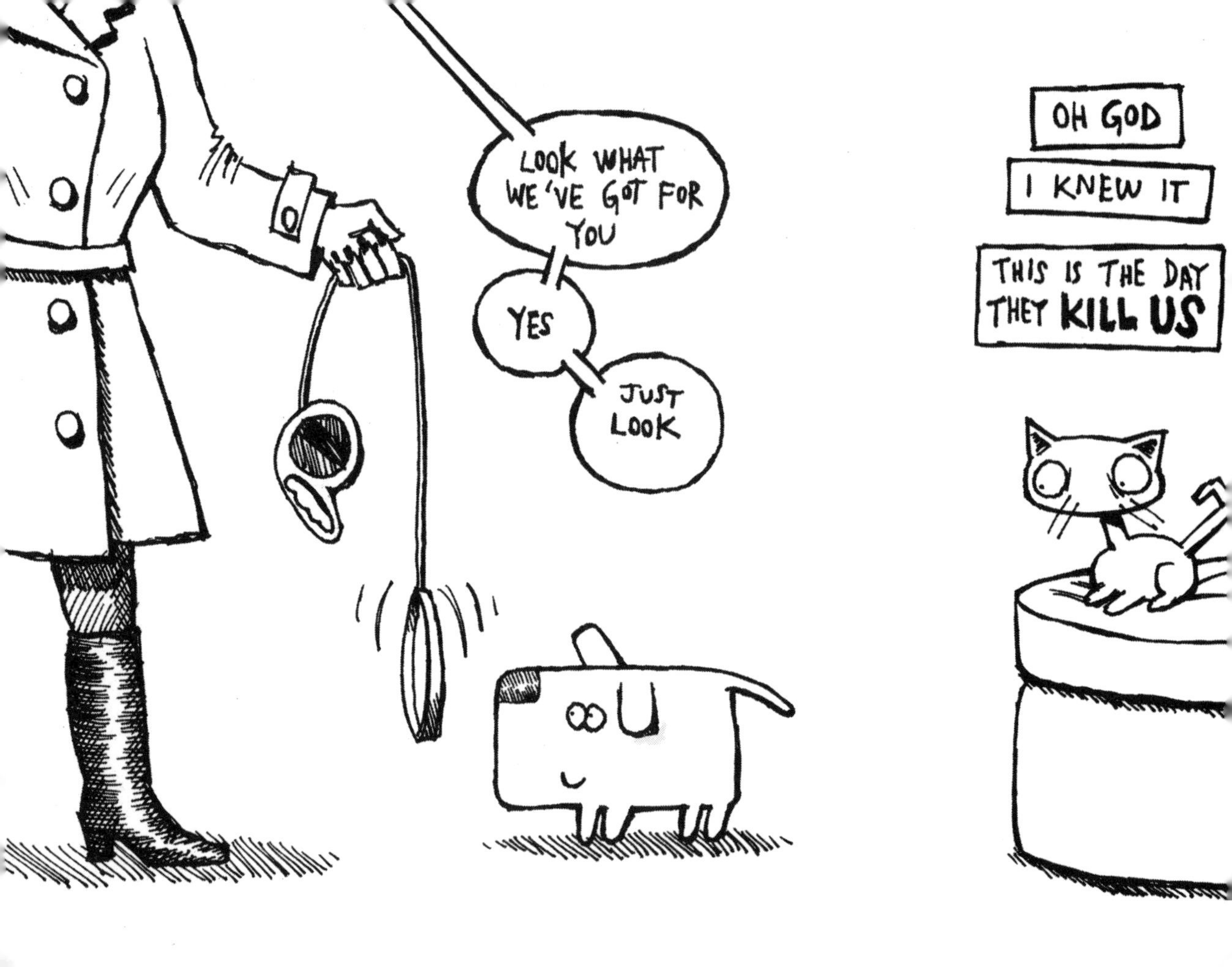
LOOK WHAT WE'VE GOT FOR YOU
YES
JUST LOOK
OH GOD
I KNEW IT
THIS IS THE DAY THEY KILL US

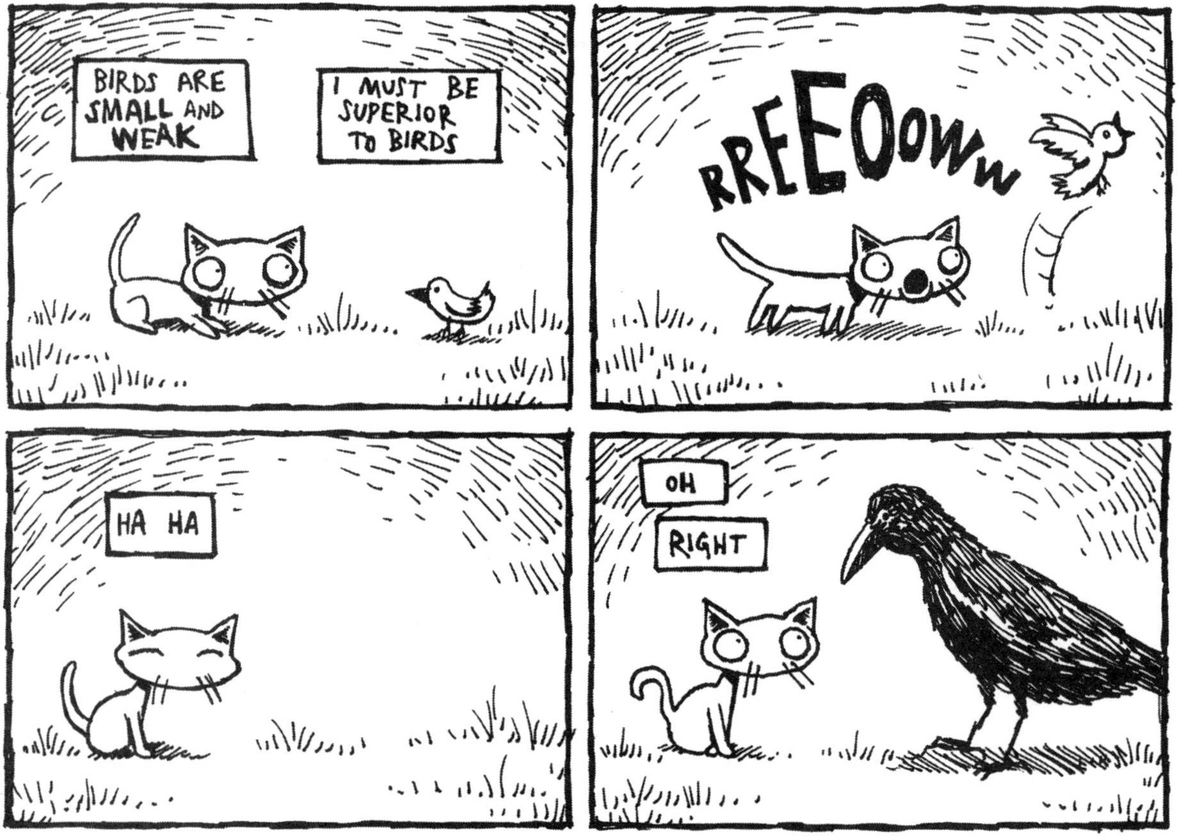
BIRDS ARE SMALL AND WEAK
I MUST BE SUPERIOR TO BIRDS
RREEOOWW
HA HA
OH
RIGHT

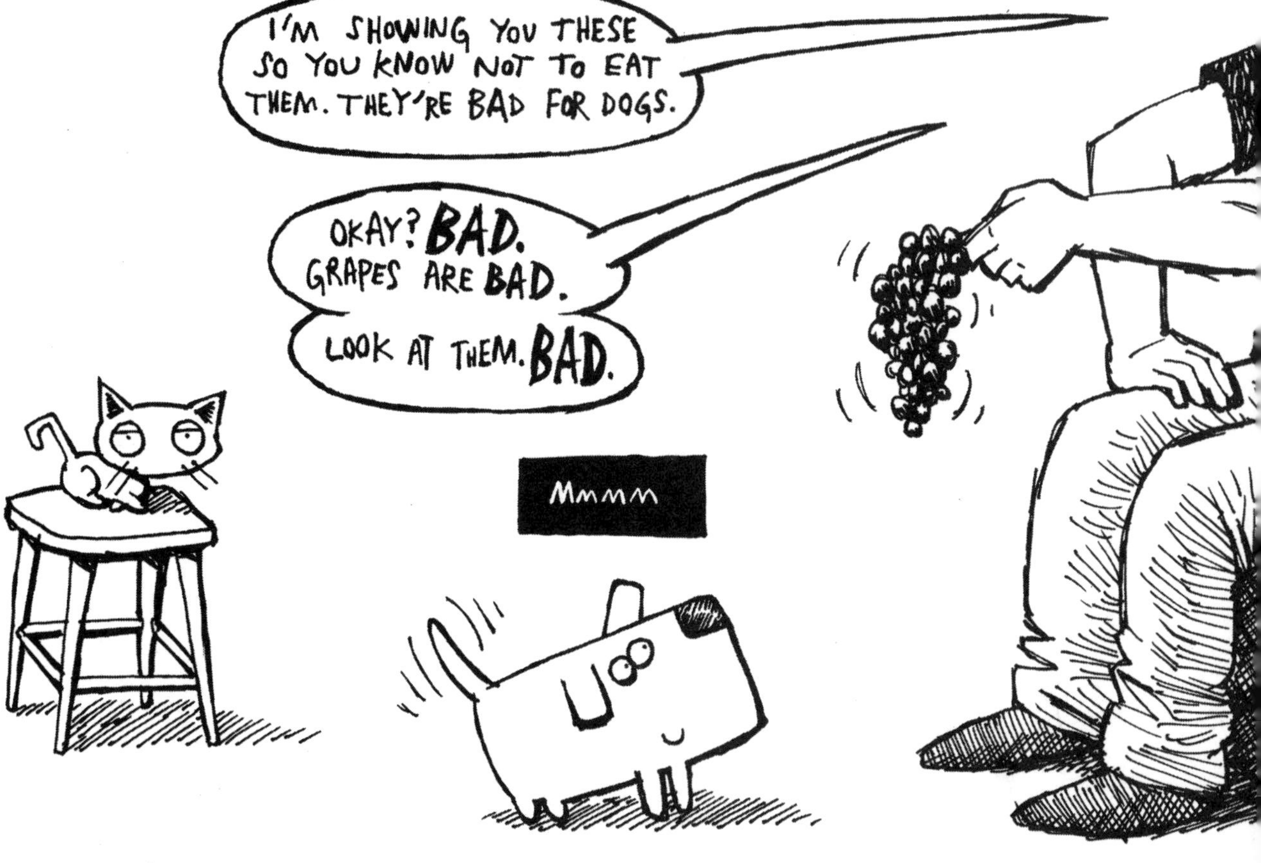
I'M SHOWING YOU THESE SO YOU KNOW NOT TO EAT THEM. THEY'RE BAD FOR DOGS.
OKAY? BAD. GRAPES ARE BAD.
LOOK AT THEM. BAD.
Mmmm

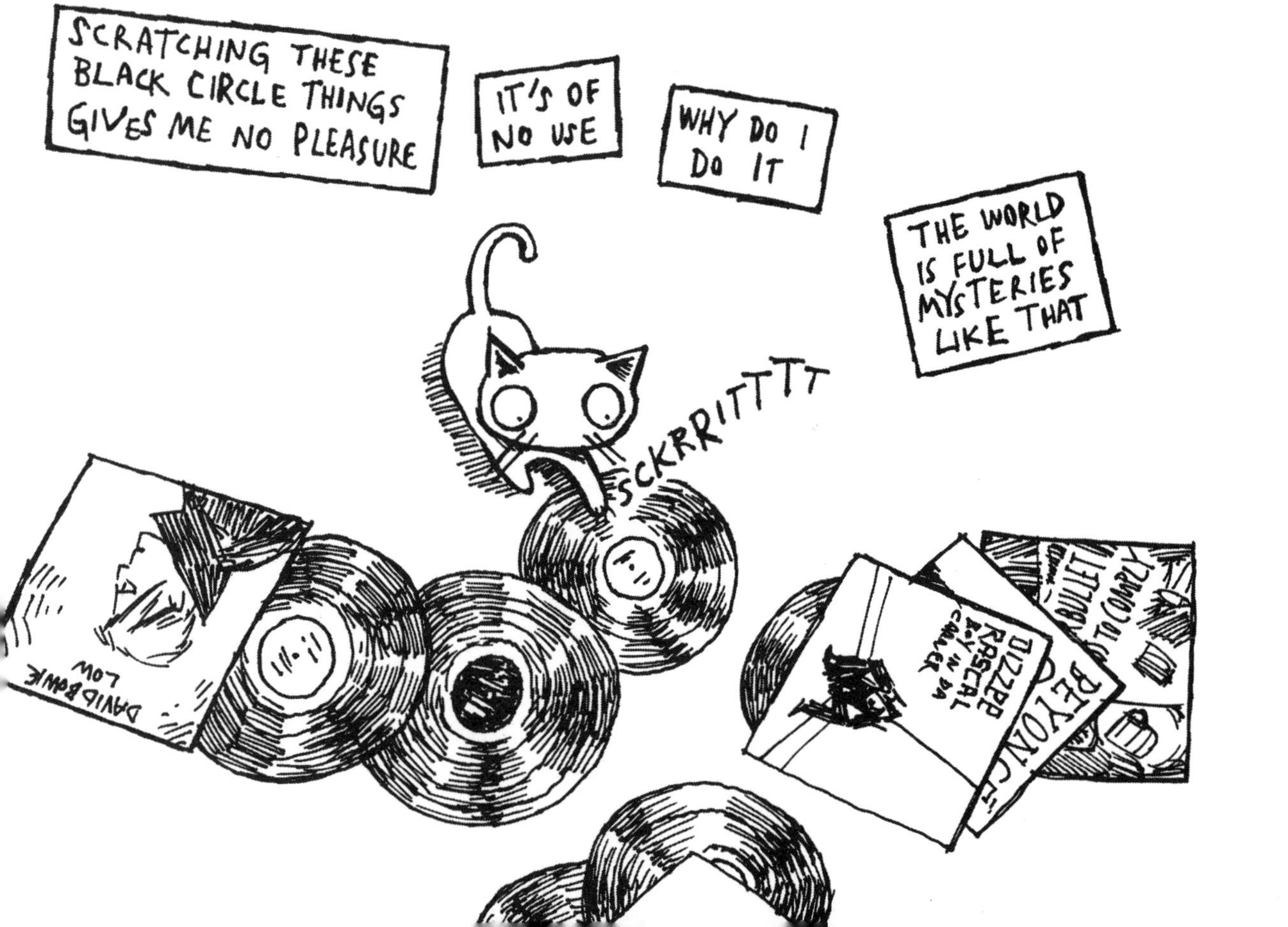
SCRATCHING THESE BLACK CIRCLE THINGS GIVES ME NO PLEASURE
IT'S OF NO USE
WHY DO I DO IT
THE WORLD IS FULL OF MYSTERIES LIKE THAT
SCKRRITTTTT
DAVID BOWIE LOW
DIZZEE RASCAL BOY IN DA CORNER
BEYONCÉ

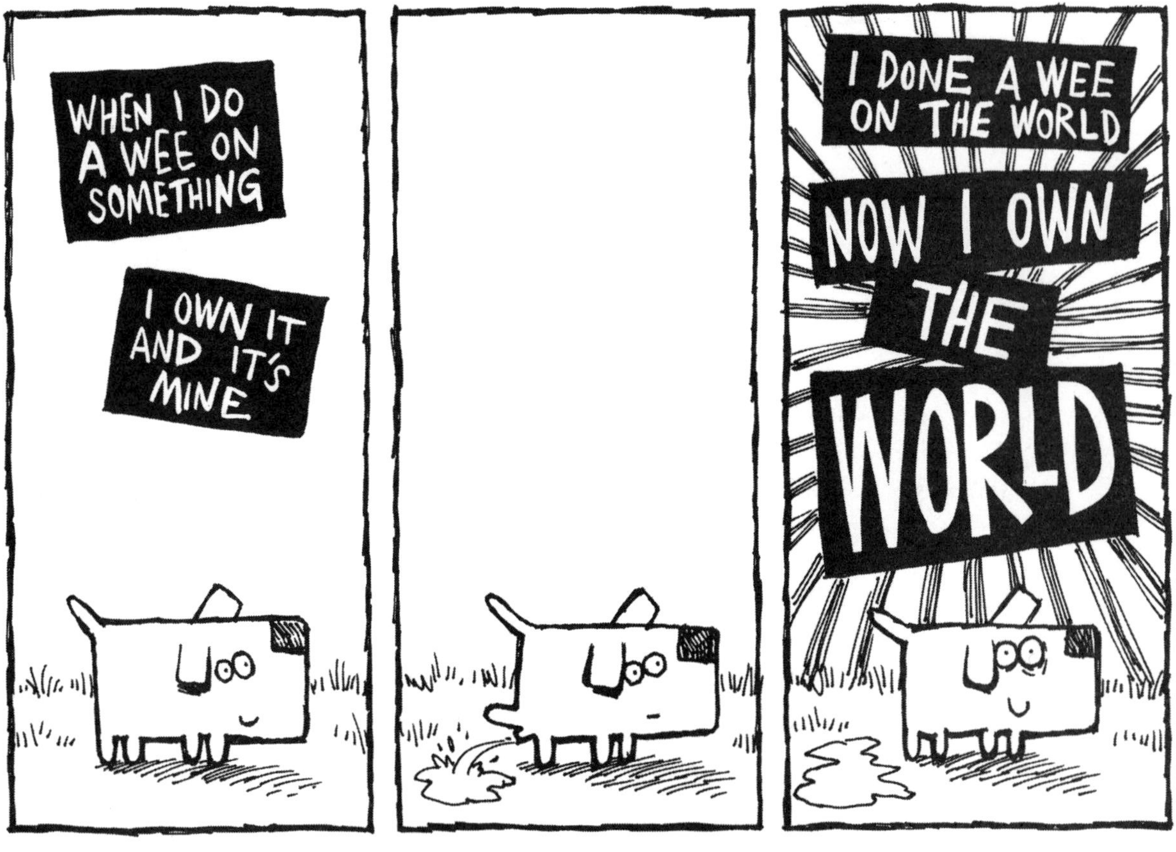
WHEN I DO A WEE ON SOMETHING
I OWN IT AND IT'S MINE
I DONE A WEE ON THE WORLD
NOW I OWN THE WORLD

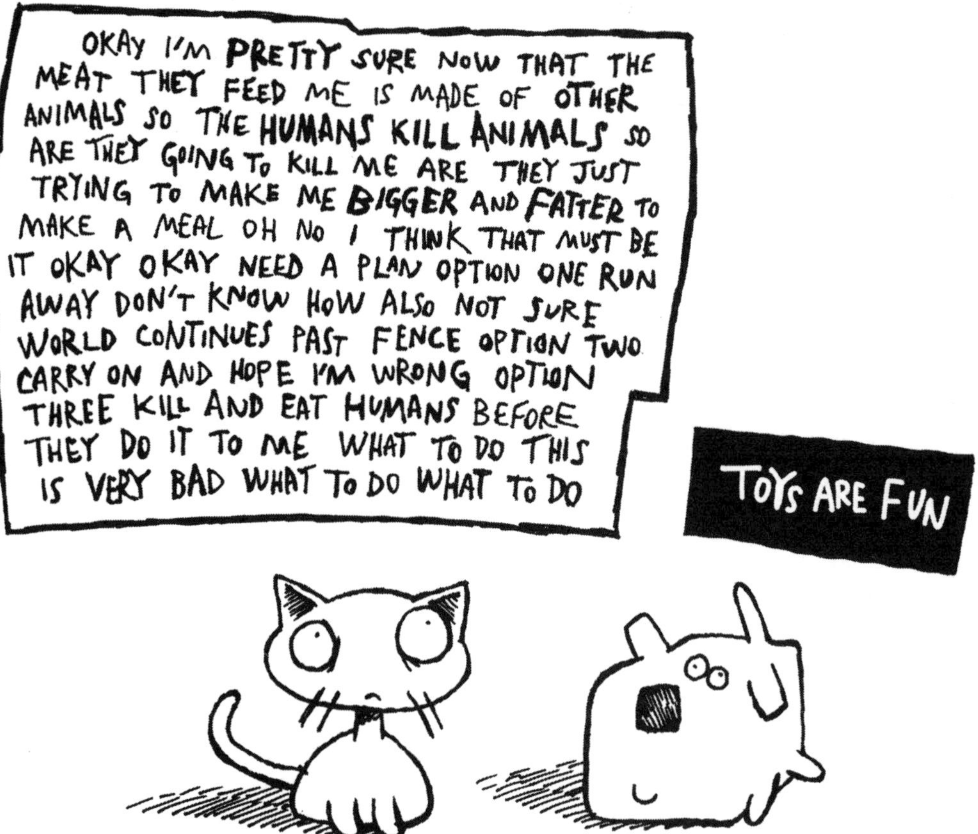
OKAY I'M PRETTY SURE NOW THAT THE MEAT THEY FEED ME IS MADE OF OTHER ANIMALS SO THE HUMANS KILL ANIMALS SO ARE THEY GOING TO KILL ME ARE THEY JUST TRYING TO MAKE ME BIGGER AND FATTER TO MAKE A MEAL OH NO I THINK THAT MUST BE IT OKAY OKAY NEED A PLAN OPTION ONE RUN AWAY DON'T KNOW HOW ALSO NOT SURE WORLD CONTINUES PAST FENCE OPTION TWO CARRY ON AND HOPE I'M WRONG OPTION THREE KILL AND EAT HUMANS BEFORE THEY DO IT TO ME WHAT TO DO THIS IS VERY BAD WHAT TO DO WHAT TO DO
TOYS ARE FUN

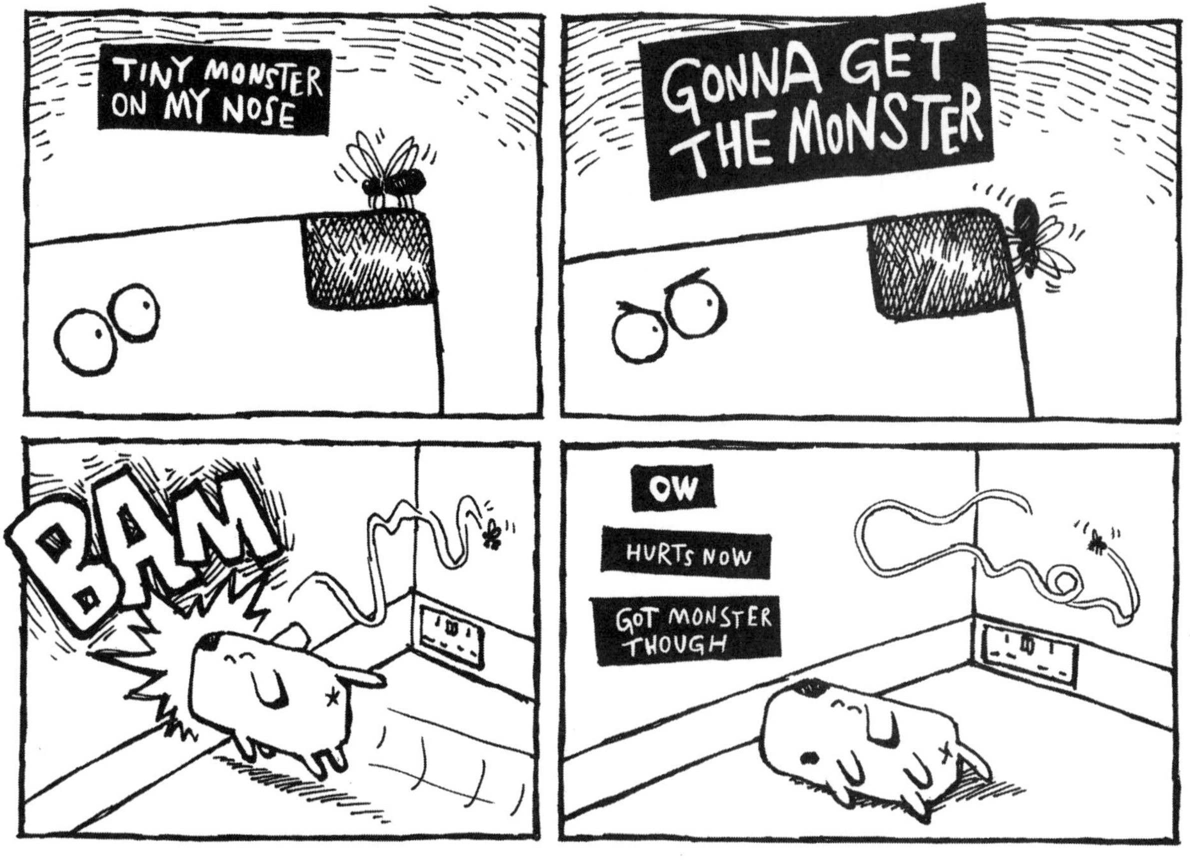
TINY MONSTER ON MY NOSE
GONNA GET THE MONSTER
BAM
OW
HURTS NOW
GOT MONSTER THOUGH

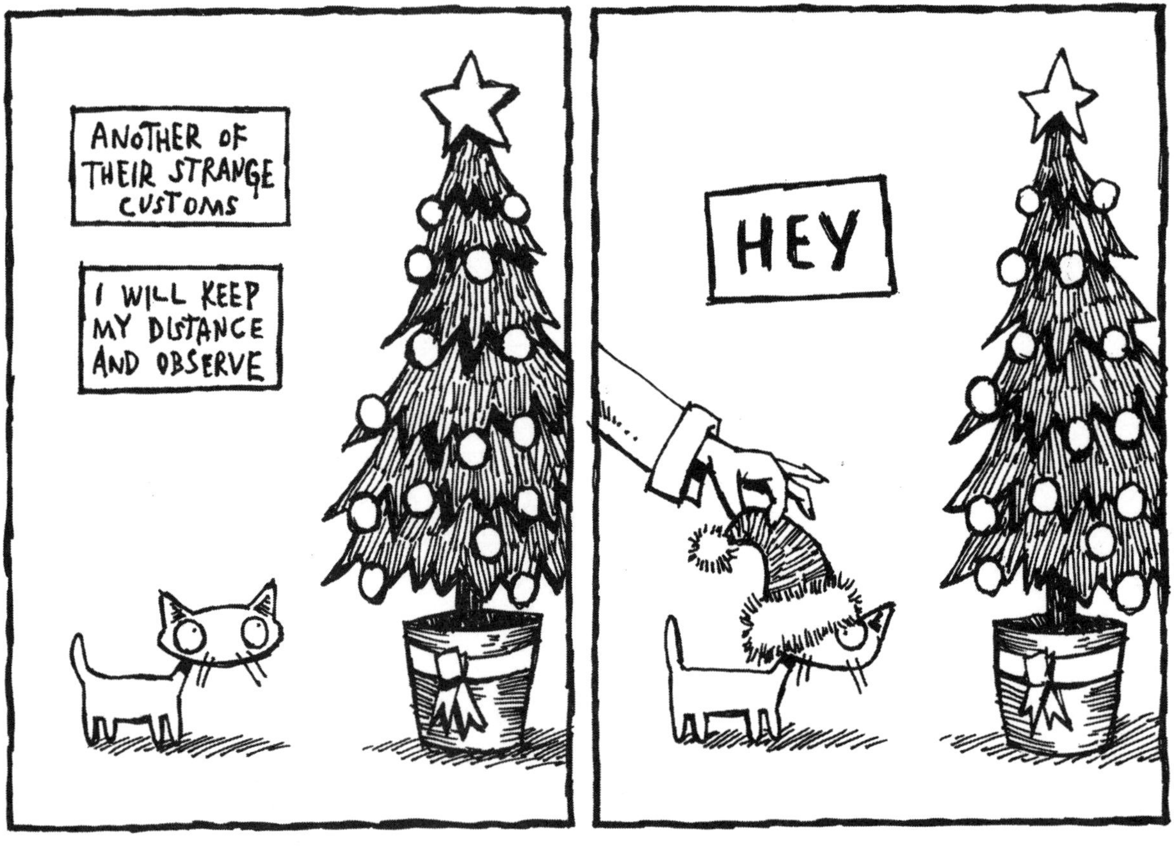
ANOTHER OF THEIR STRANGE CUSTOMS
I WILL KEEP MY DISTANCE AND OBSERVE
HEY

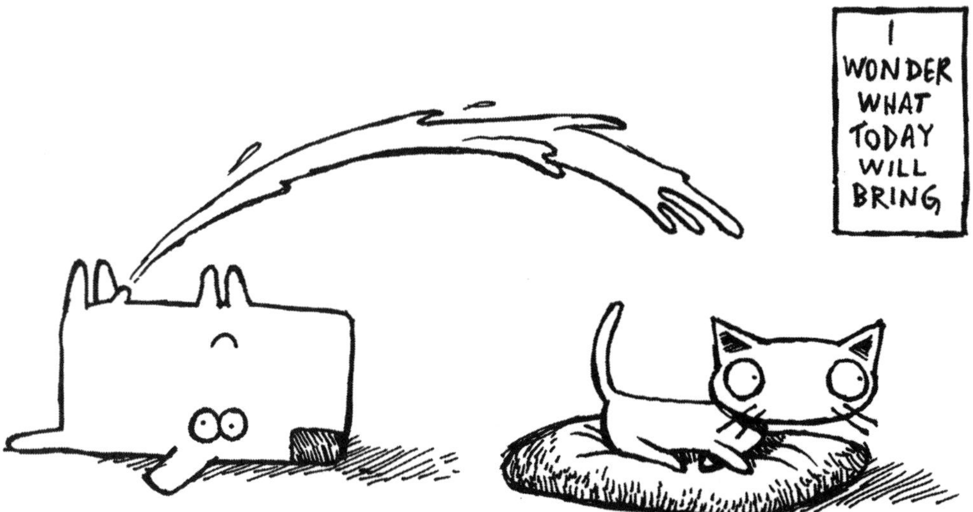
I WONDER WHAT TODAY WILL BRING

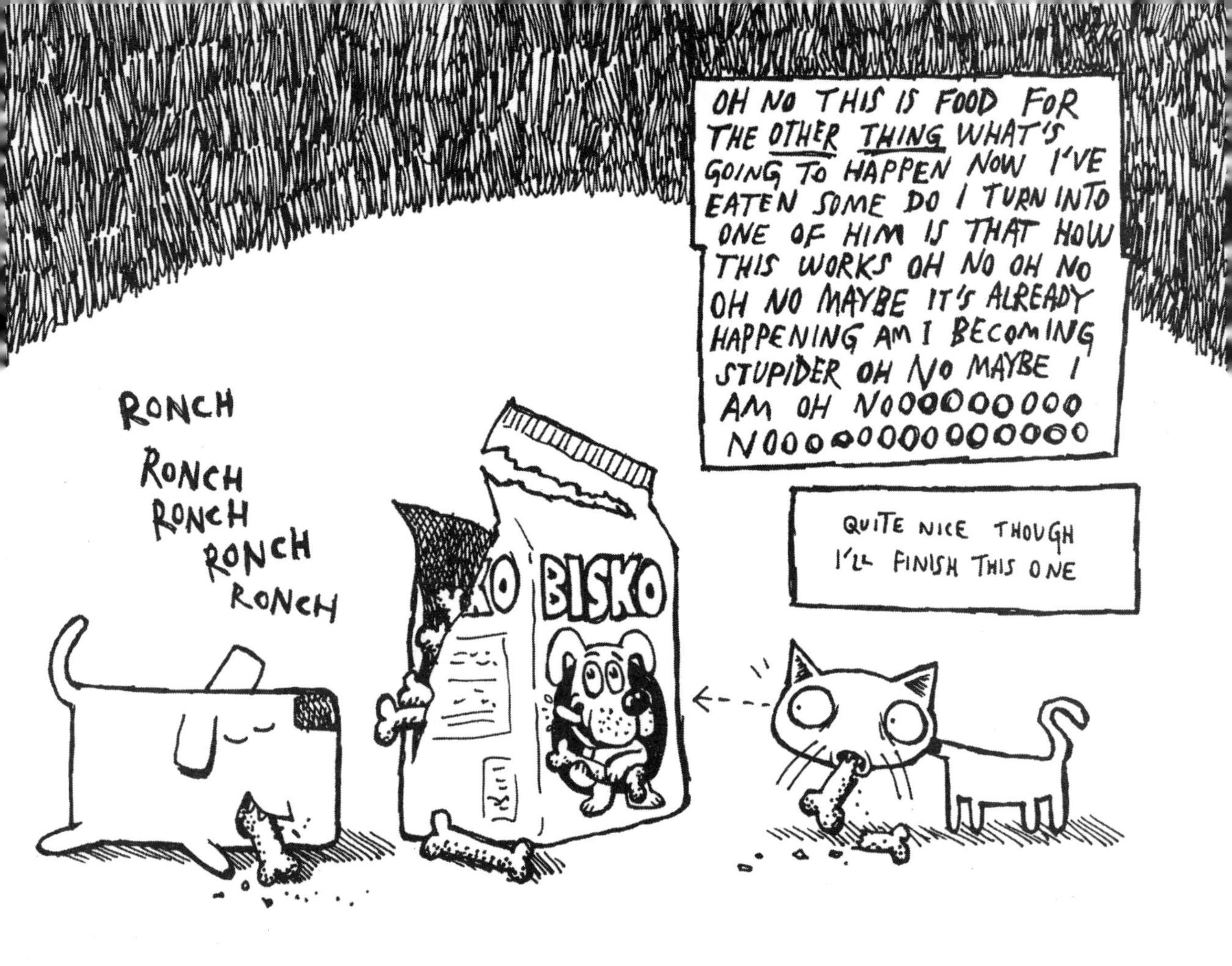
OH NO THIS IS FOOD FOR THE OTHER THING WHAT'S GOING TO HAPPEN NOW I'VE EATEN SOME DO I TURN INTO ONE OF HIM IS THAT HOW THIS WORKS OH NO OH NO OH NO MAYBE IT'S ALREADY HAPPENING AM I BECOMING STUPIDER OH NO MAYBE I AM OH NOOOOOOOOO NOOOOOOOOOOOOOOO
RONCH
RONCH
RONCH
RONCH
RONCH
BISKO
QUITE NICE THOUGH I'LL FINISH THIS ONE

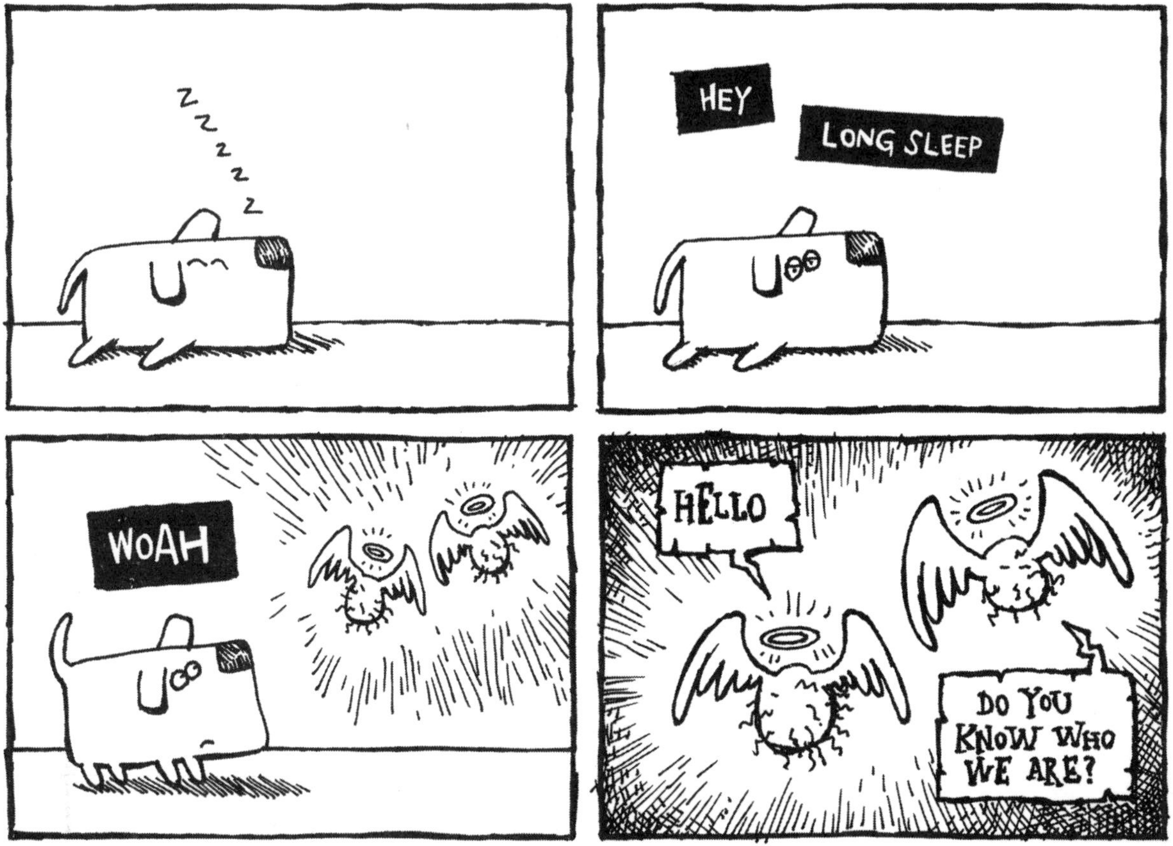
Z Z Z Z Z
HEY
LONG SLEEP
WOAH
HELLO
DO YOU KNOW WHO WE ARE?

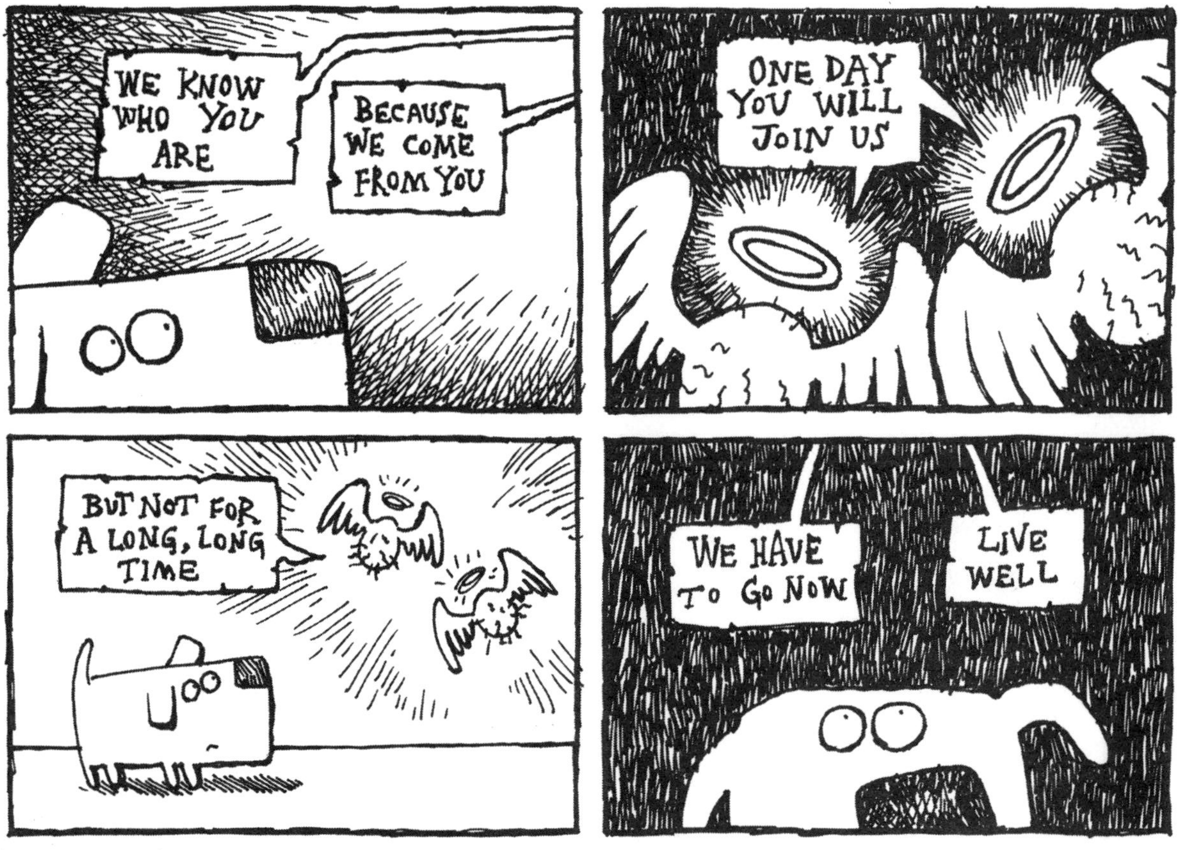
WE KNOW WHO YOU ARE
BECAUSE WE COME FROM YOU
ONE DAY YOU WILL JOIN US
BUT NOT FOR A LONG, LONG TIME
WE HAVE TO GO NOW
LIVE WELL

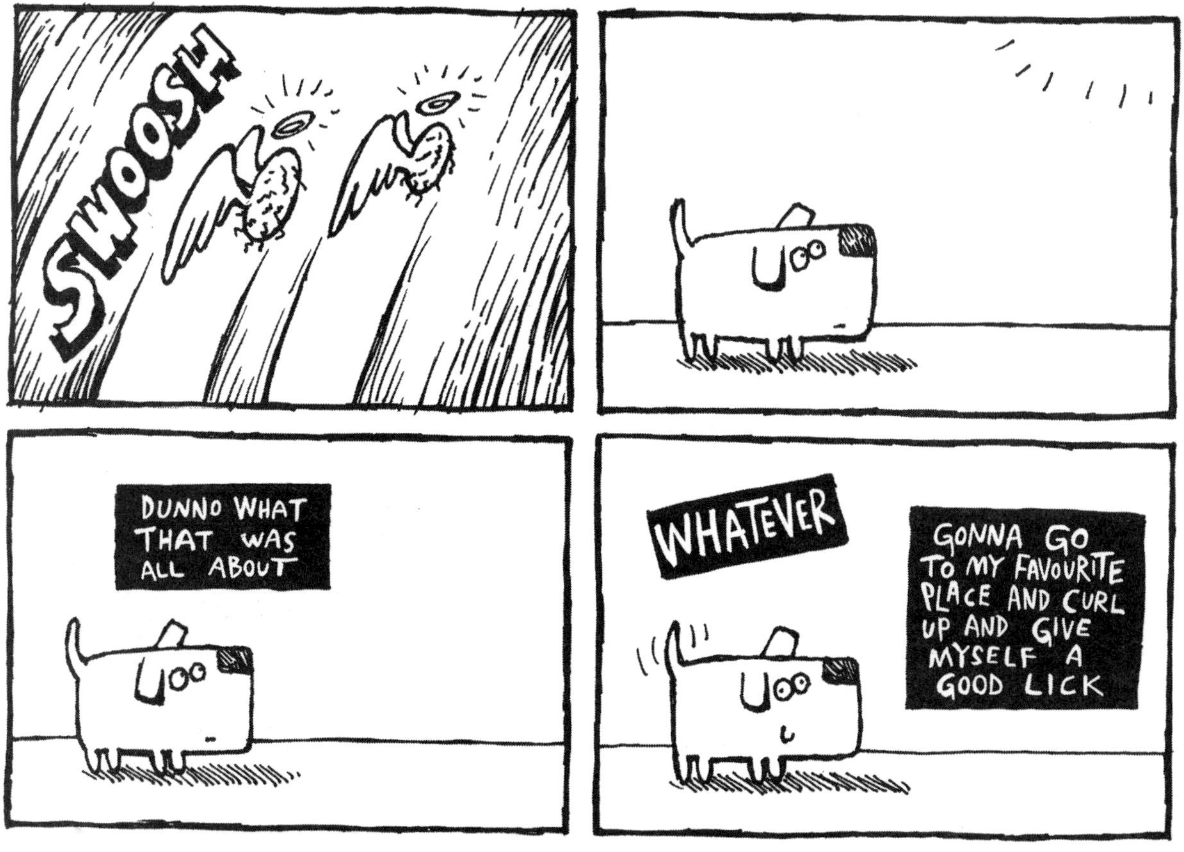
SWOOSH
DUNNO WHAT THAT WAS ALL ABOUT
WHATEVER
GONNA GO TO MY FAVOURITE PLACE AND CURL UP AND GIVE MYSELF A GOOD LICK

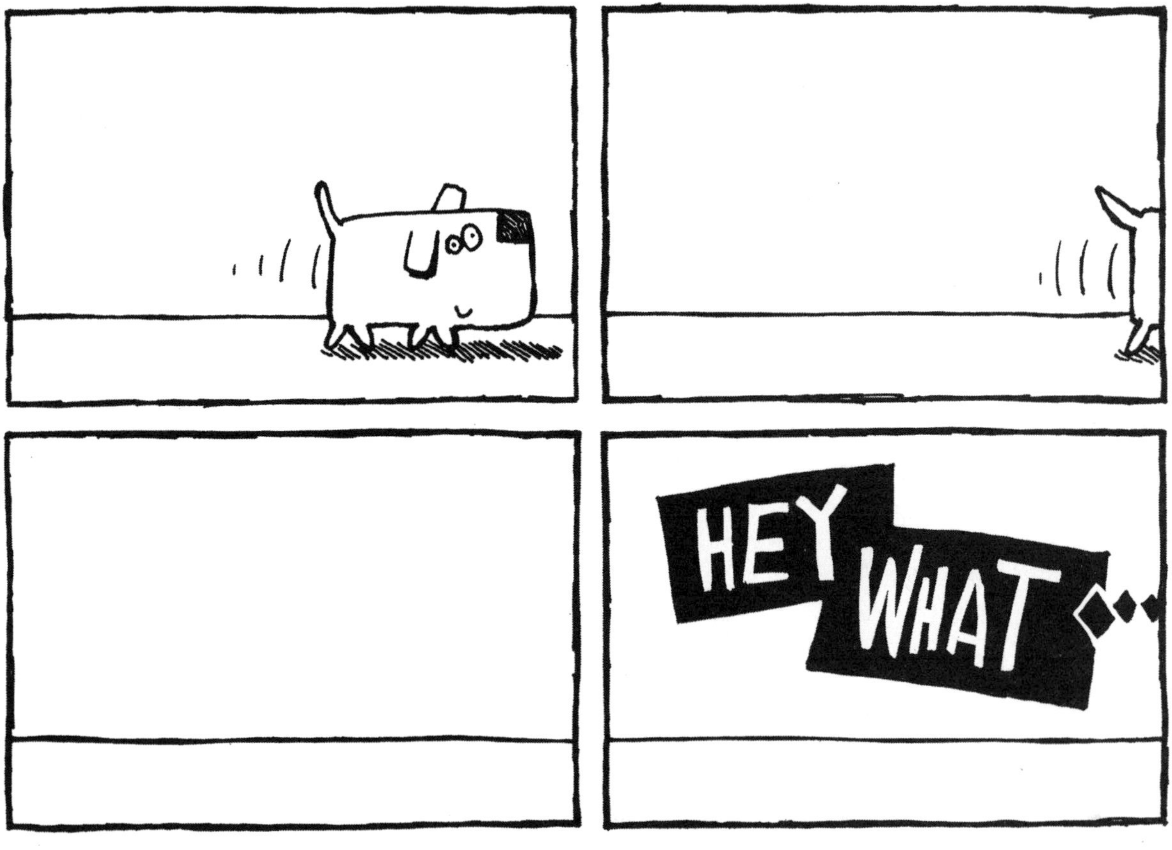
HEY WHAT

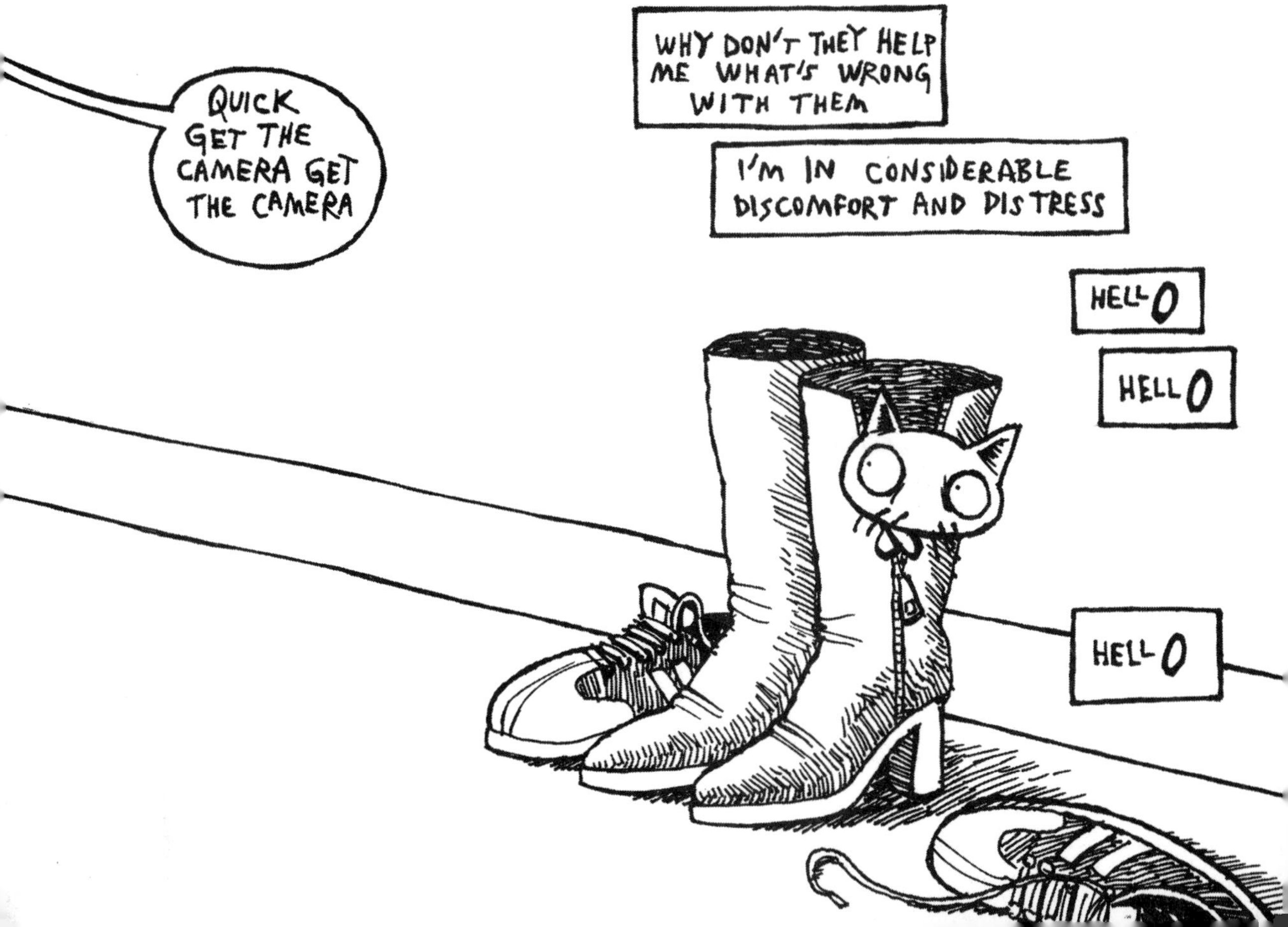
QUICK GET THE CAMERA GET THE CAMERA
WHY DON'T THEY HELP ME WHAT'S WRONG WITH THEM
I'M IN CONSIDERABLE DISCOMFORT AND DISTRESS
HELLO
HELLO
HELLO

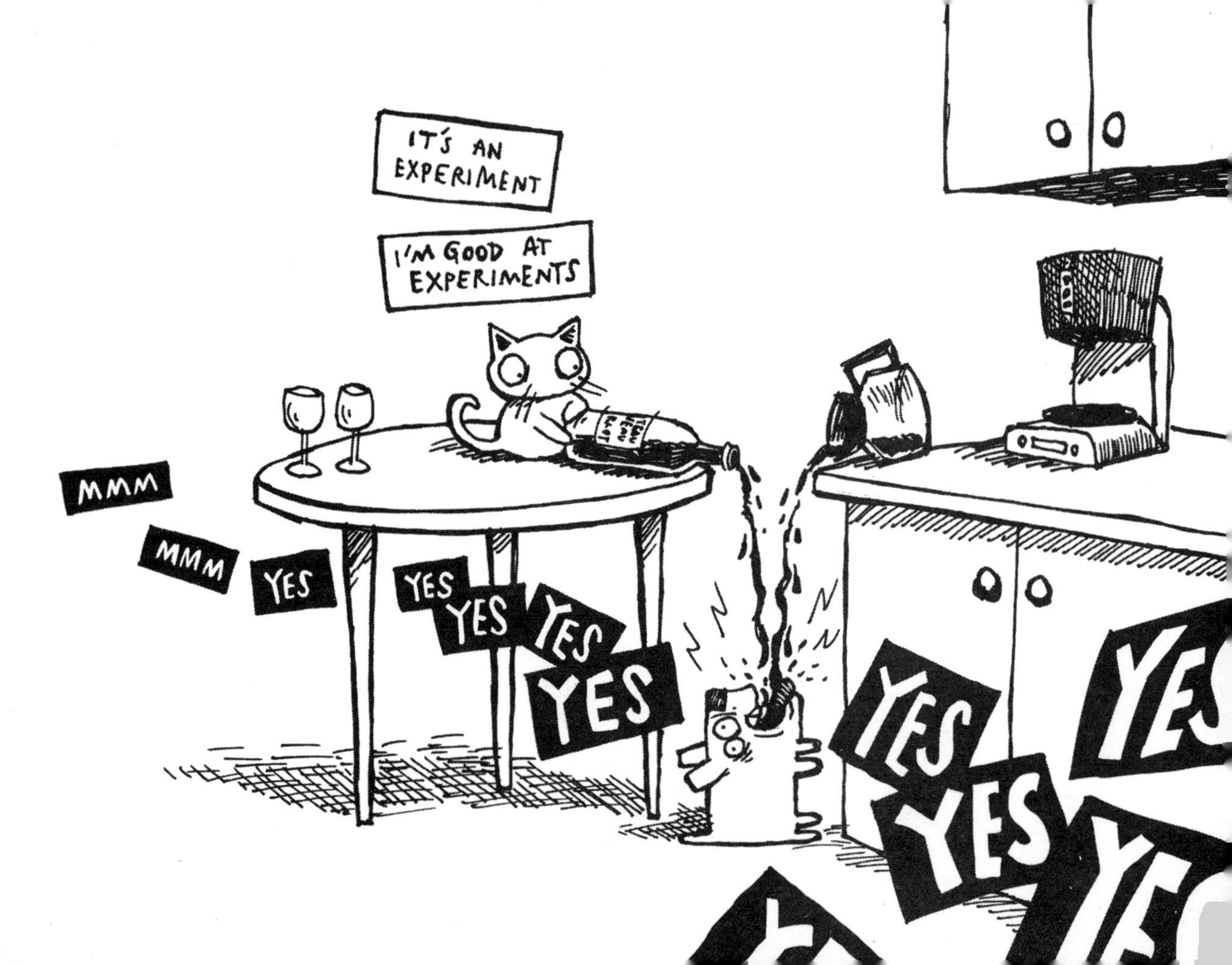
IT'S AN EXPERIMENT
I'M GOOD AT EXPERIMENTS
MMM
MMM
YES
YES
YES
YES
YES
YES
YES

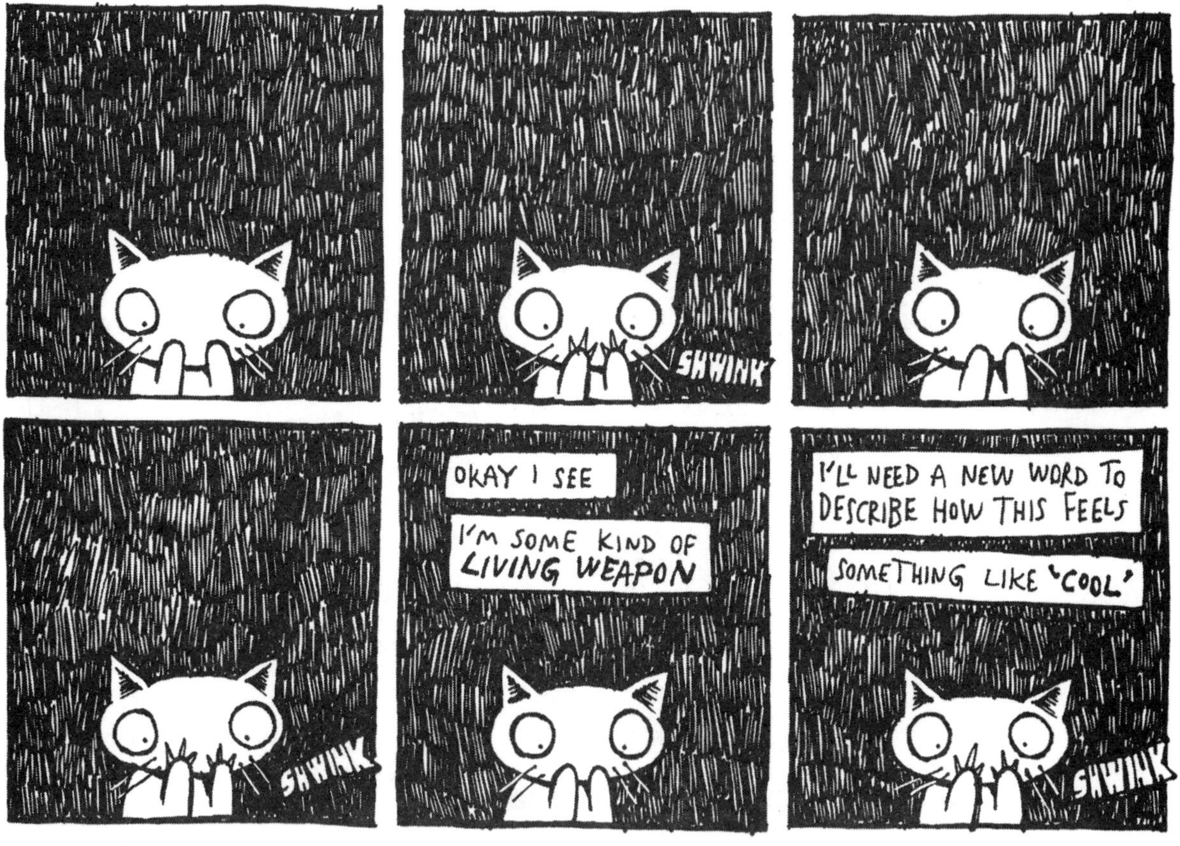
SHWINK
SHWINK
OKAY I SEE
I'M SOME KIND OF LIVING WEAPON
I'LL NEED A NEW WORD TO DESCRIBE HOW THIS FEELS
SOMETHING LIKE 'COOL'
SHWINK

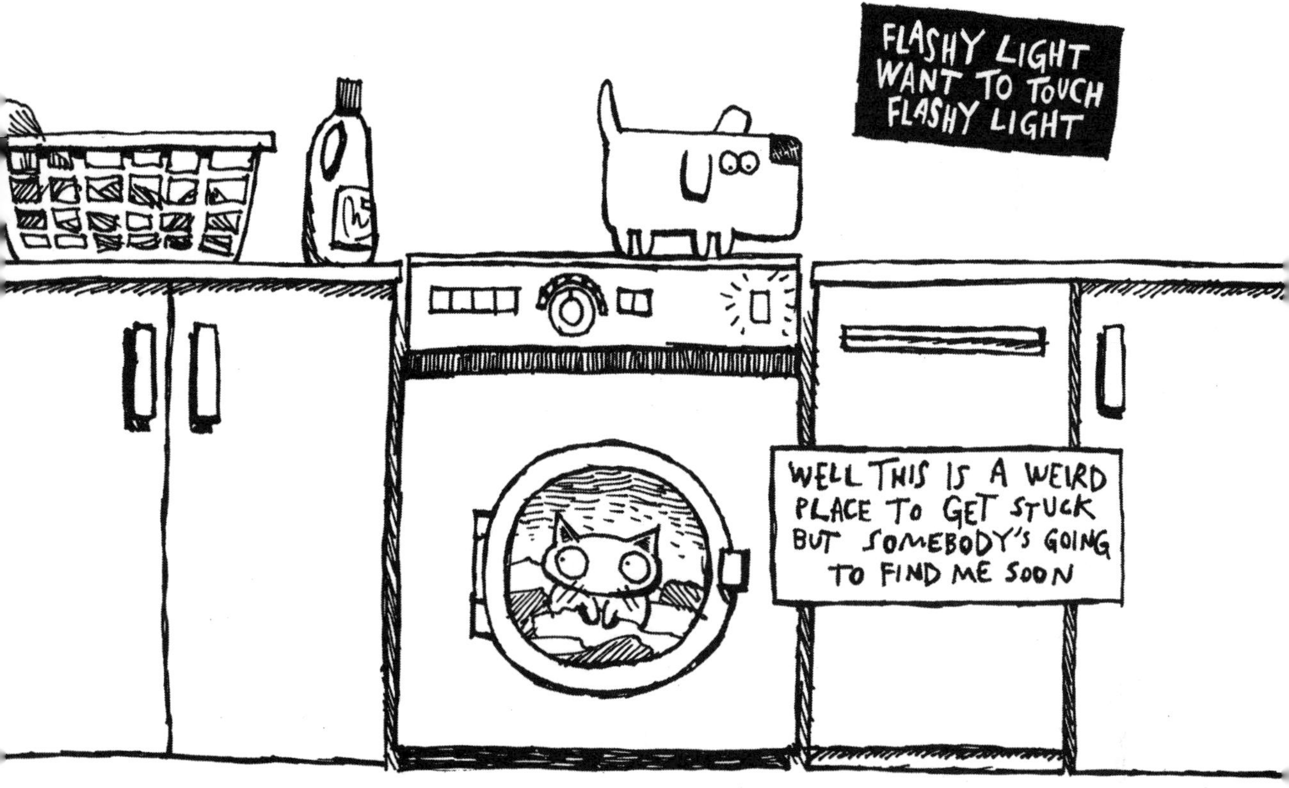
FLASHY LIGHT
WANT TO TOUCH
FLASHY LIGHT
WELL THIS IS A WEIRD
PLACE TO GET STUCK
BUT SOMEBODY'S GOING
TO FIND ME SOON

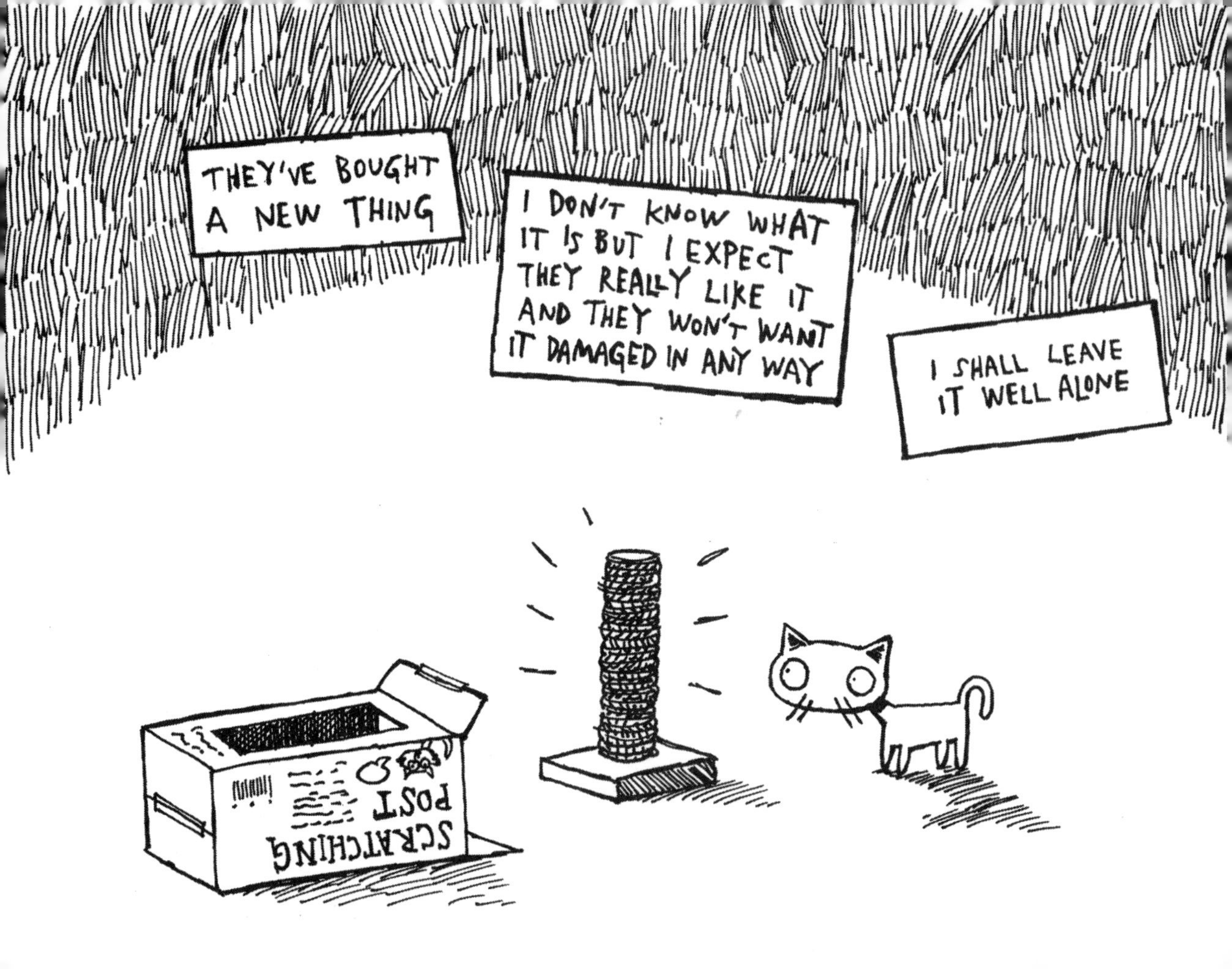
THEY'VE BOUGHT A NEW THING
I DON'T KNOW WHAT IT IS BUT I EXPECT THEY REALLY LIKE IT AND THEY WON'T WANT IT DAMAGED IN ANY WAY
I SHALL LEAVE IT WELL ALONE
SCRATCHING POST

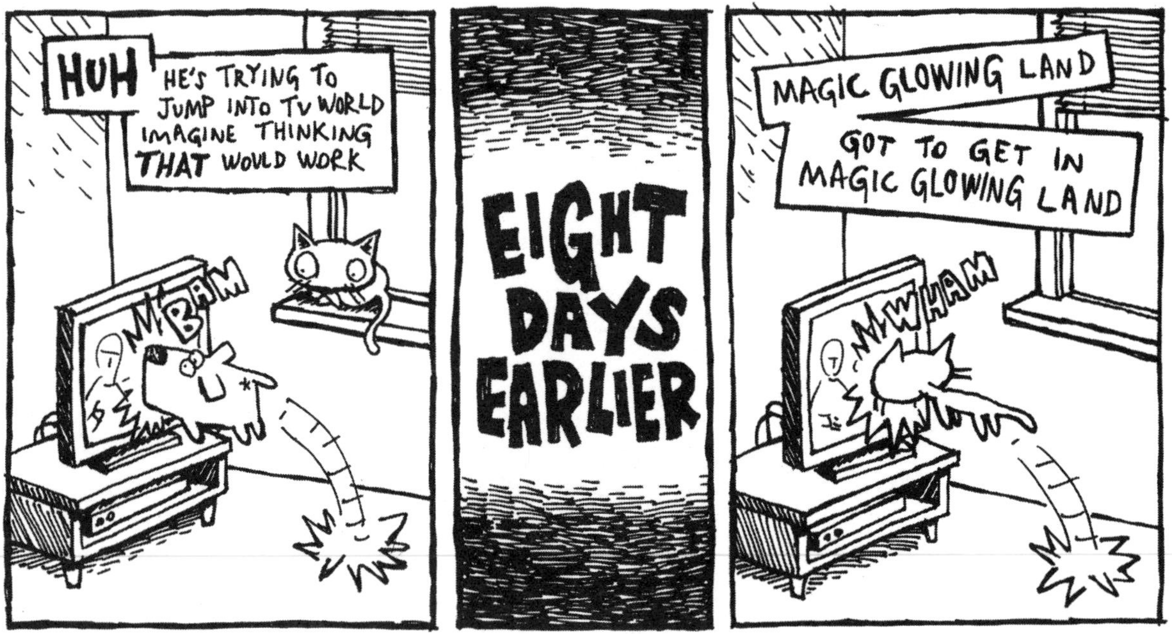
HUH
HE'S TRYING TO JUMP INTO TV WORLD IMAGINE THINKING THAT WOULD WORK
BAM
EIGHT DAYS EARLIER
MAGIC GLOWING LAND
GOT TO GET IN MAGIC GLOWING LAND
WHAM

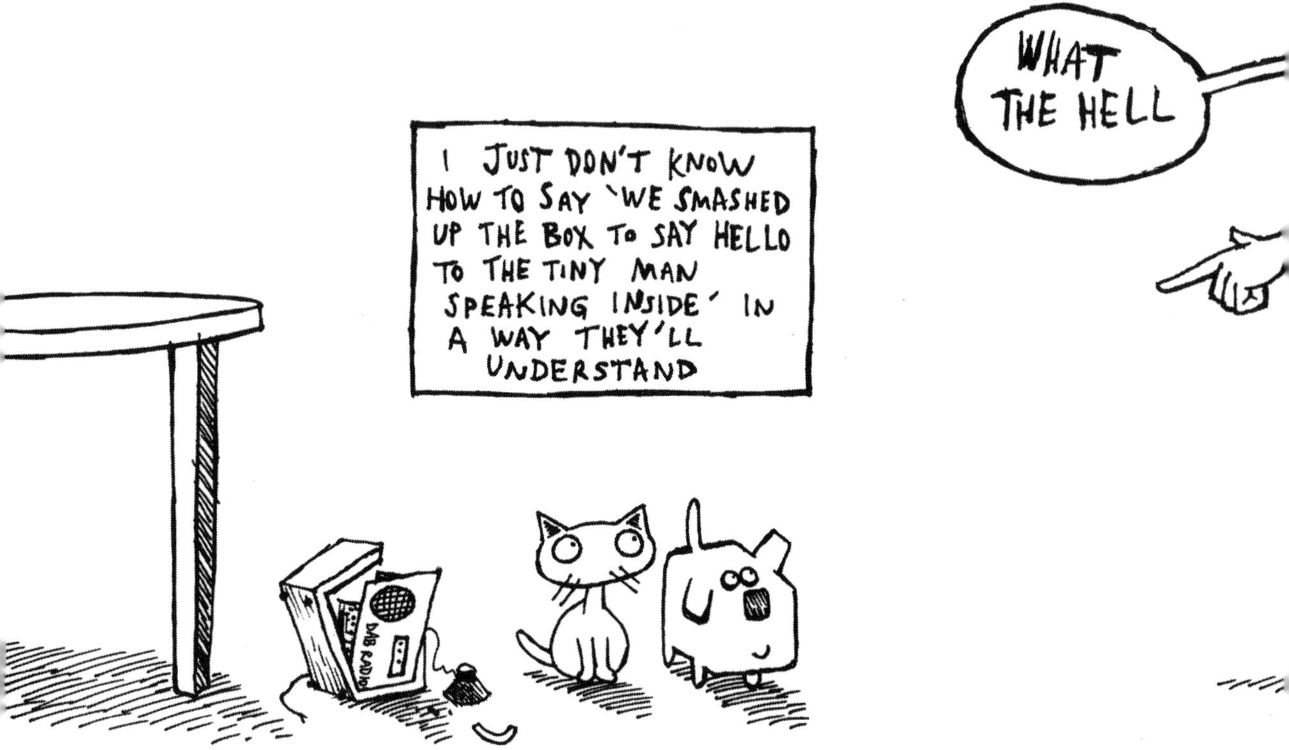
I JUST DON'T KNOW HOW TO SAY 'WE SMASHED UP THE BOX TO SAY HELLO TO THE TINY MAN SPEAKING INSIDE' IN A WAY THEY'LL UNDERSTAND
WHAT THE HELL
DAB RADIO

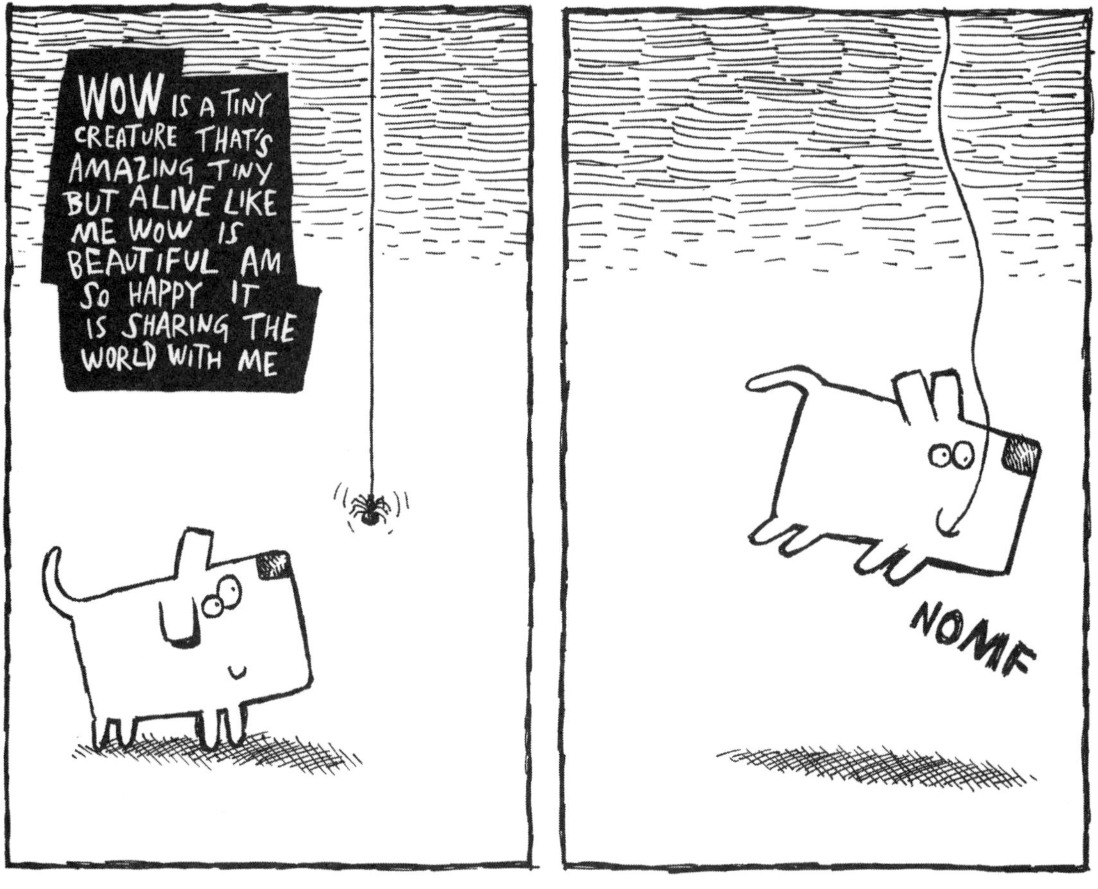
WOW IS A TINY CREATURE THAT'S AMAZING TINY BUT ALIVE LIKE ME WOW IS BEAUTIFUL AM SO HAPPY IT IS SHARING THE WORLD WITH ME
NOMF

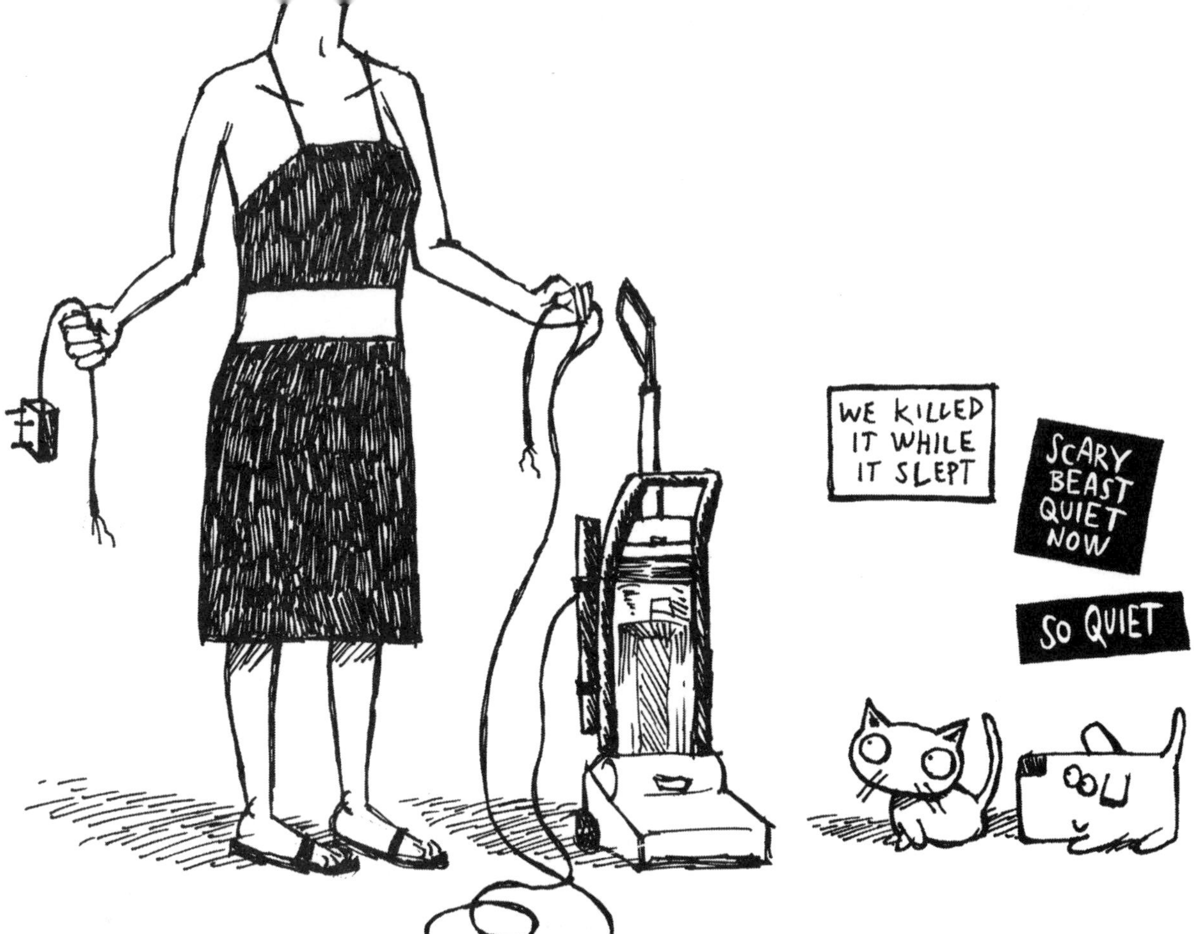
WE KILLED IT WHILE IT SLEPT
SCARY BEAST QUIET NOW
SO QUIET

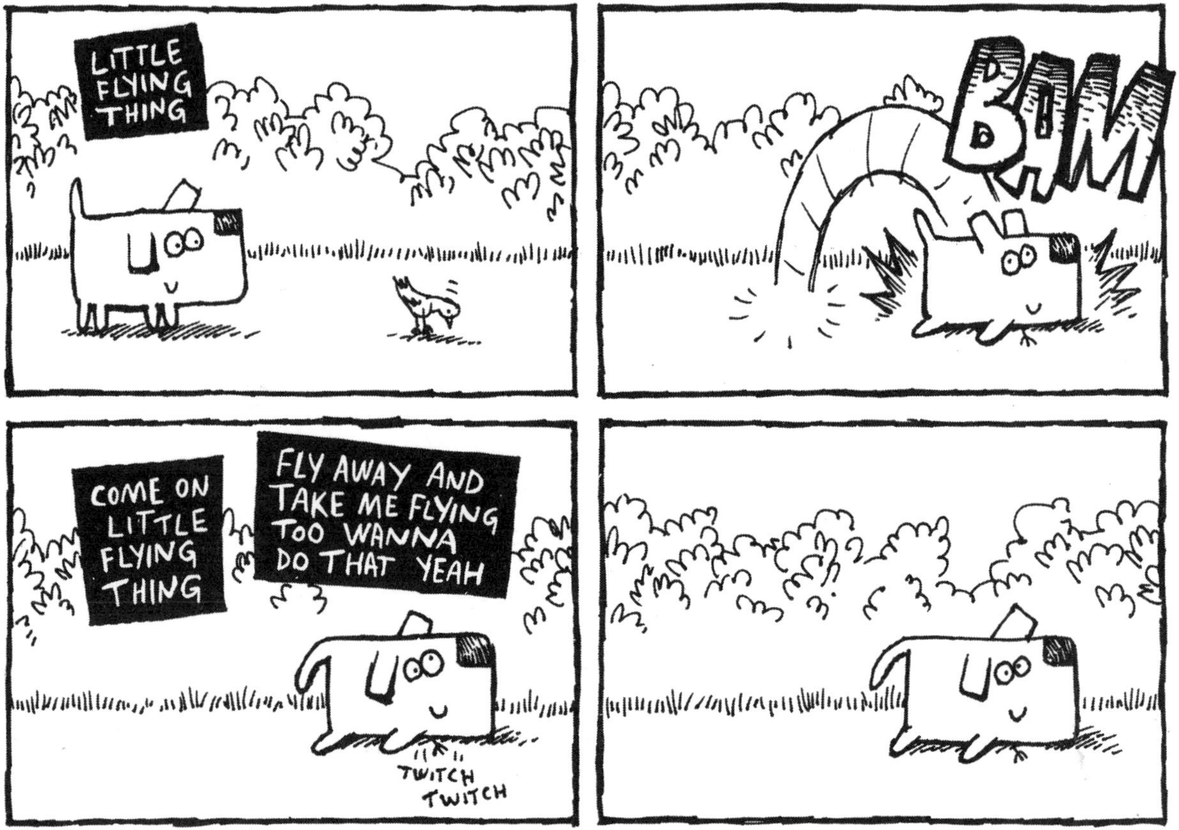
LITTLE FLYING THING
BAM
COME ON LITTLE FLYING THING
FLY AWAY AND TAKE ME FLYING TOO WANNA DO THAT YEAH
TWITCH TWITCH

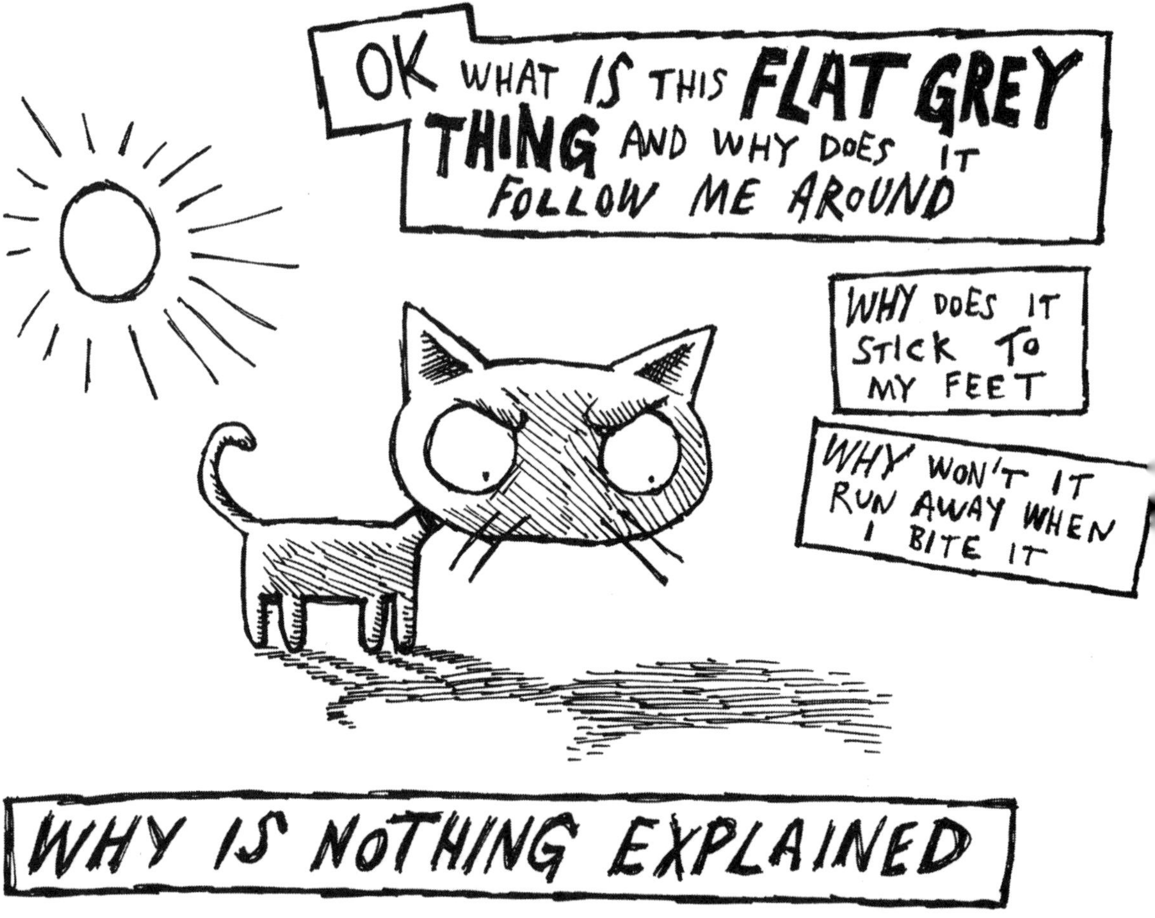
OK WHAT IS THIS FLAT GREY THING AND WHY DOES IT FOLLOW ME AROUND
WHY DOES IT STICK TO MY FEET
WHY WON'T IT RUN AWAY WHEN I BITE IT
WHY IS NOTHING EXPLAINED

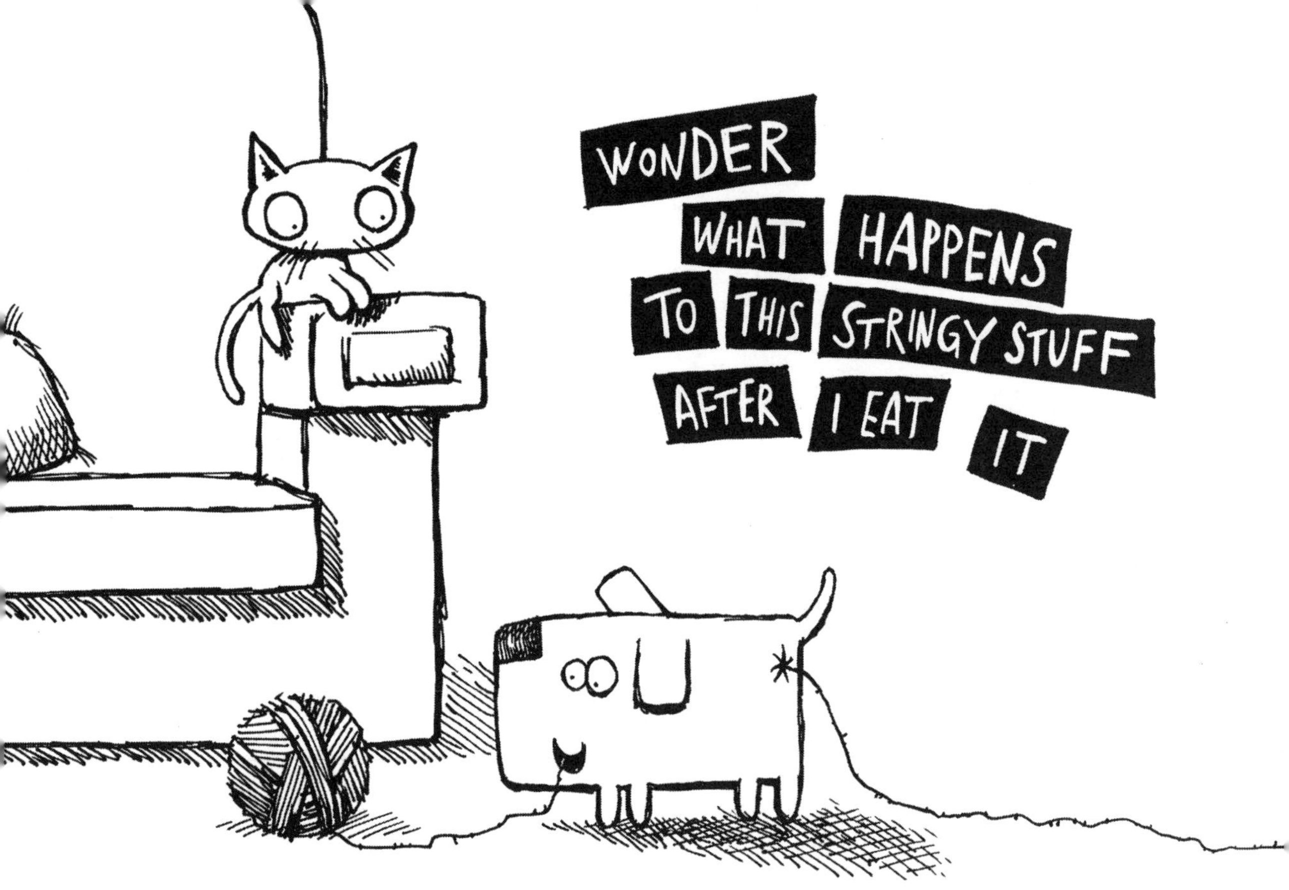
WONDER WHAT HAPPENS TO THIS STRINGY STUFF AFTER I EAT IT

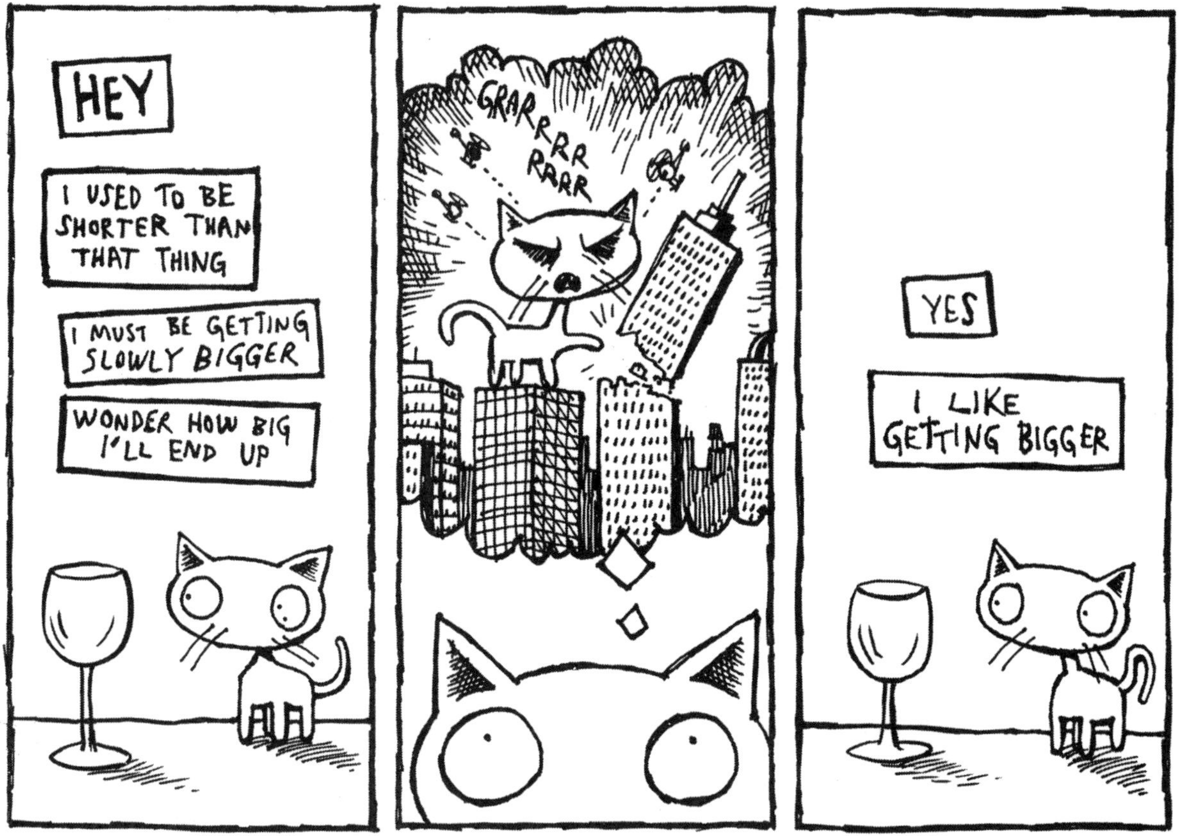
HEY
I USED TO BE SHORTER THAN THAT THING
I MUST BE GETTING SLOWLY BIGGER
WONDER HOW BIG I'LL END UP
GRARRRRR RRRR
YES
I LIKE GETTING BIGGER

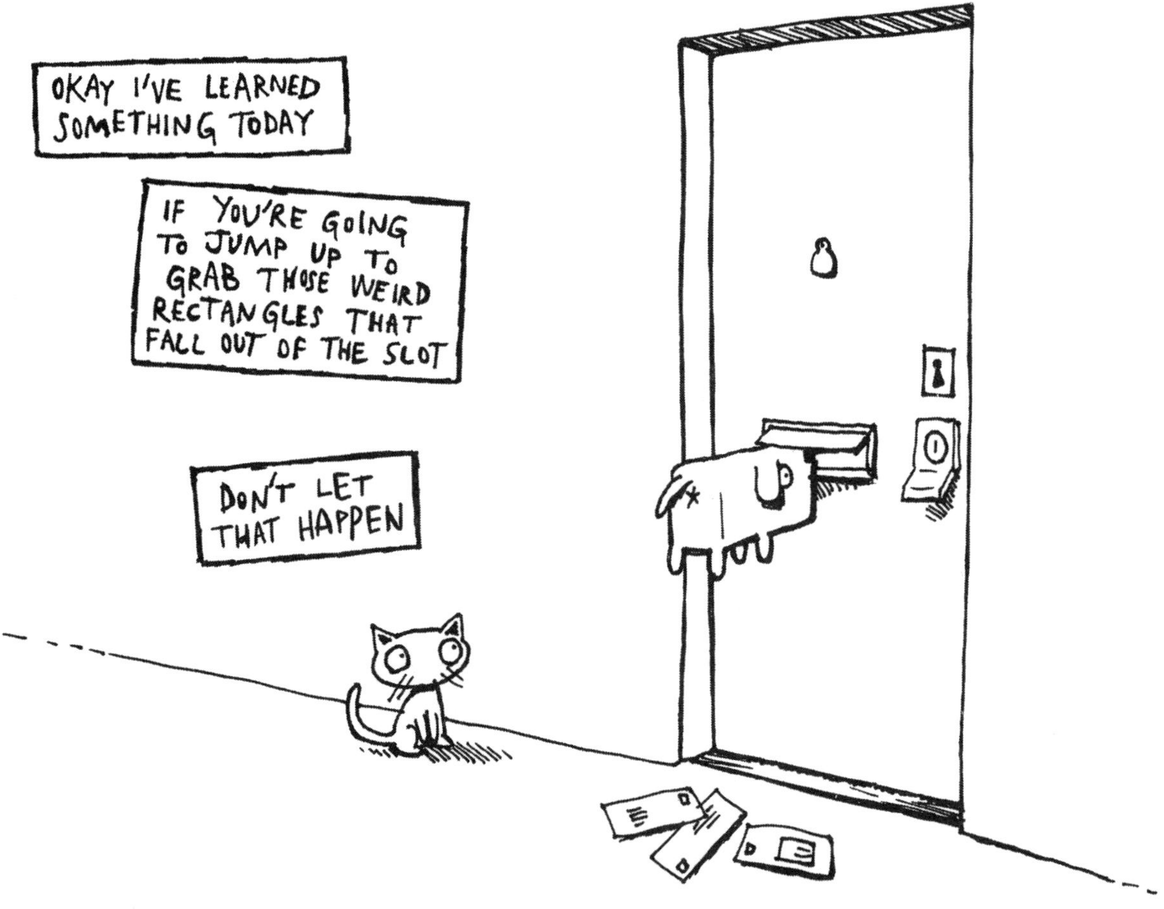
OKAY I'VE LEARNED SOMETHING TODAY
IF YOU'RE GOING TO JUMP UP TO GRAB THOSE WEIRD RECTANGLES THAT FALL OUT OF THE SLOT
DON'T LET THAT HAPPEN

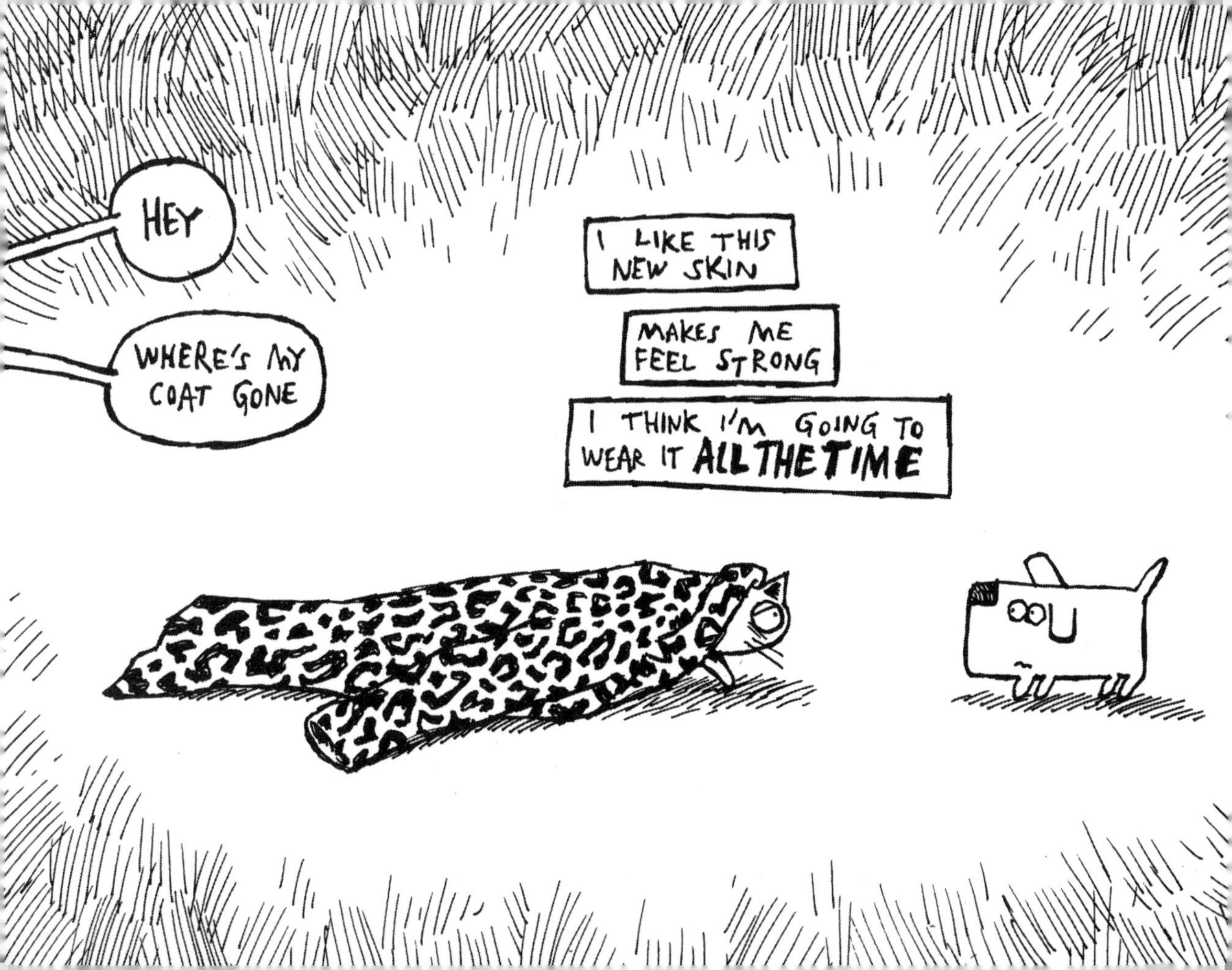
HEY
WHERE'S MY COAT GONE
I LIKE THIS NEW SKIN
MAKES ME FEEL STRONG
I THINK I'M GOING TO WEAR IT ALL THE TIME

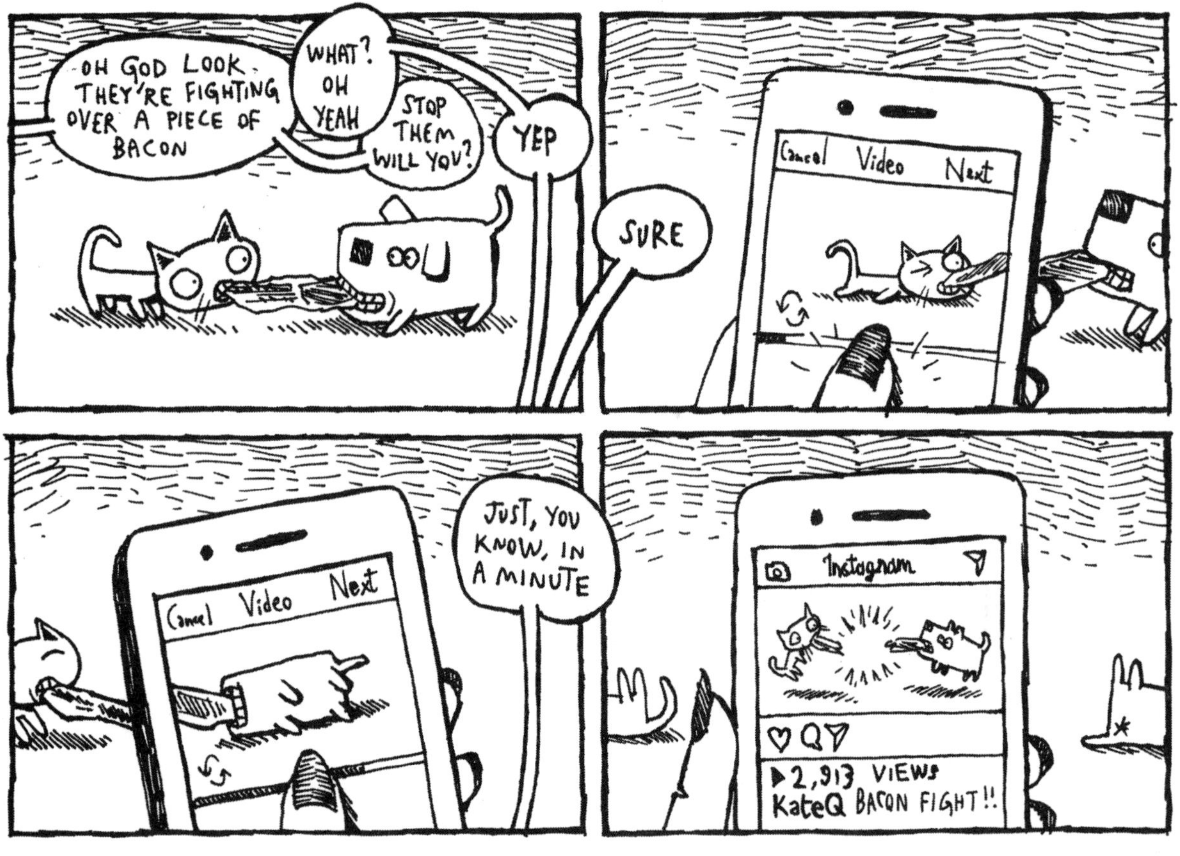
OH GOD LOOK THEY'RE FIGHTING OVER A PIECE OF BACON
WHAT? OH YEAH
STOP THEM WILL YOU?
YEP
SURE
Cancel Video Next
Cancel Video Next
JUST, YOU KNOW, IN A MINUTE
Instagram
▶2,913 VIEWS
KateQ BACON FIGHT!!

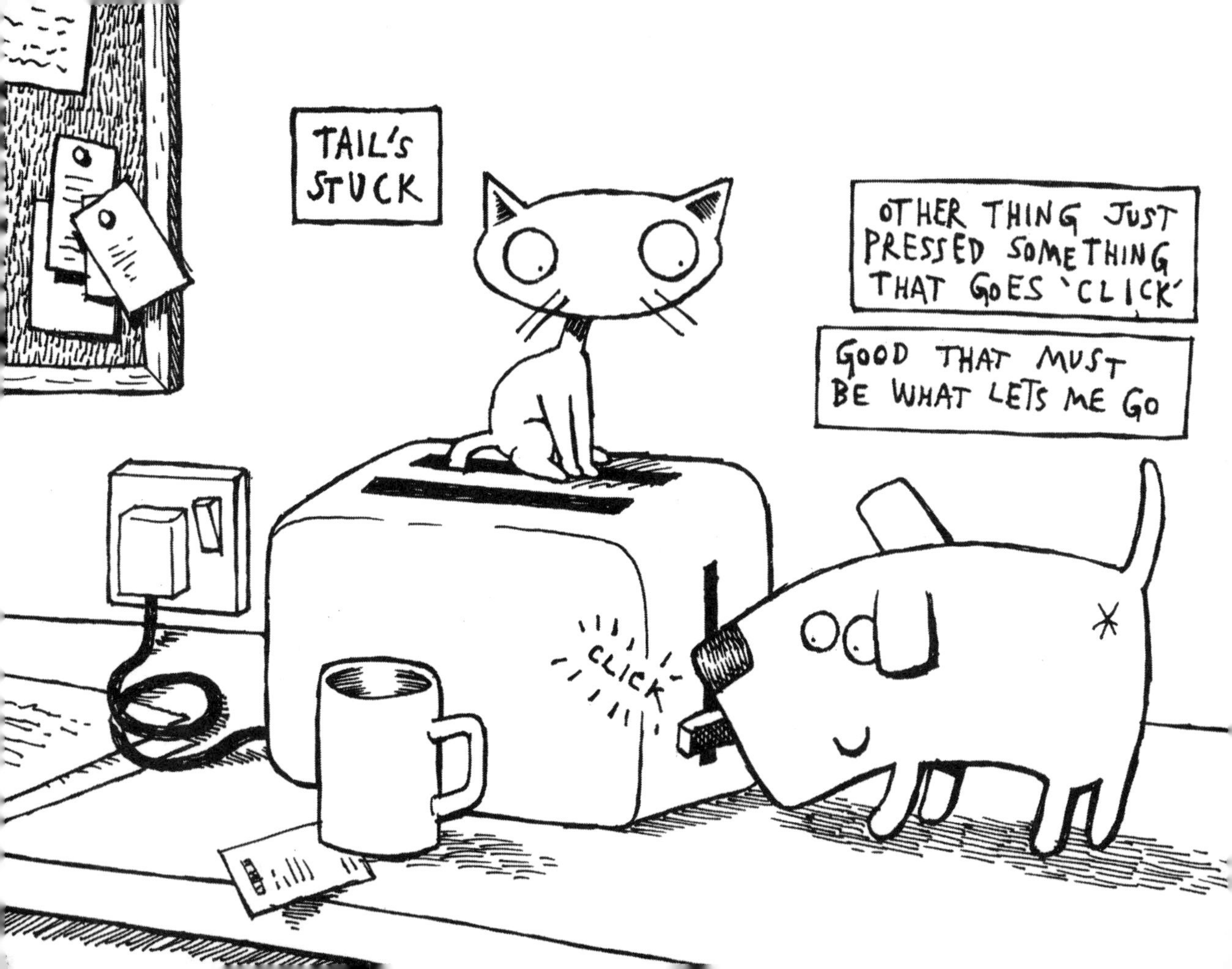
TAIL'S STUCK
OTHER THING JUST PRESSED SOMETHING THAT GOES 'CLICK'
GOOD THAT MUST BE WHAT LETS ME GO
CLICK

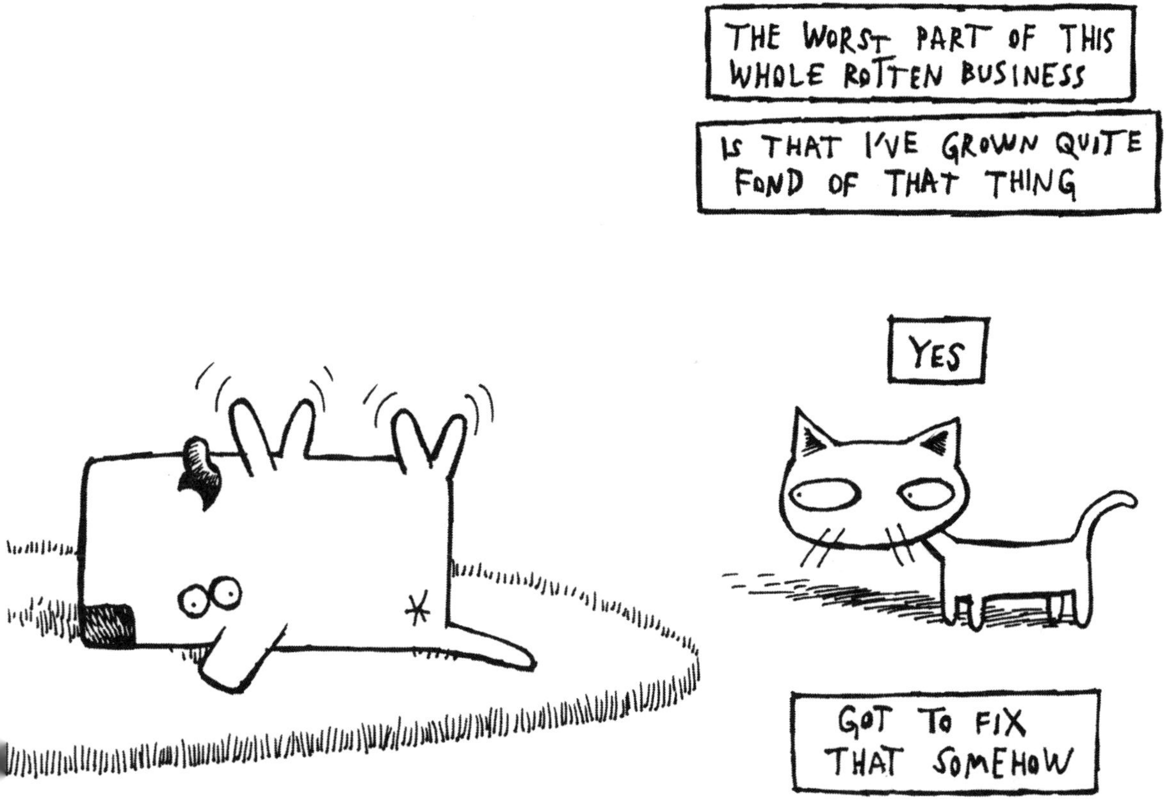
THE WORST PART OF THIS WHOLE ROTTEN BUSINESS
IS THAT I'VE GROWN QUITE FOND OF THAT THING
YES
GOT TO FIX THAT SOMEHOW

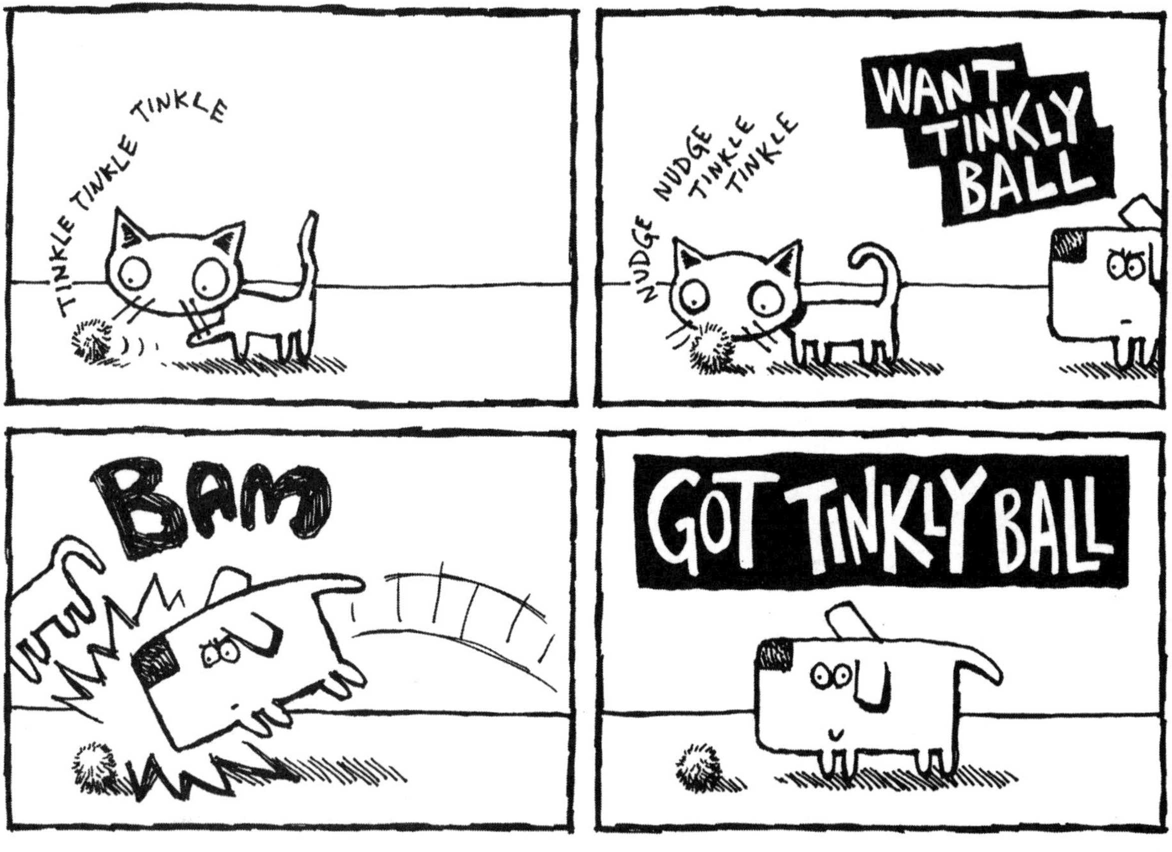

TINKLE TINKLE TINKLE
NUDGE NUDGE TINKLE TINKLE
WANT TINKLY BALL
BAM
GOT TINKLY BALL

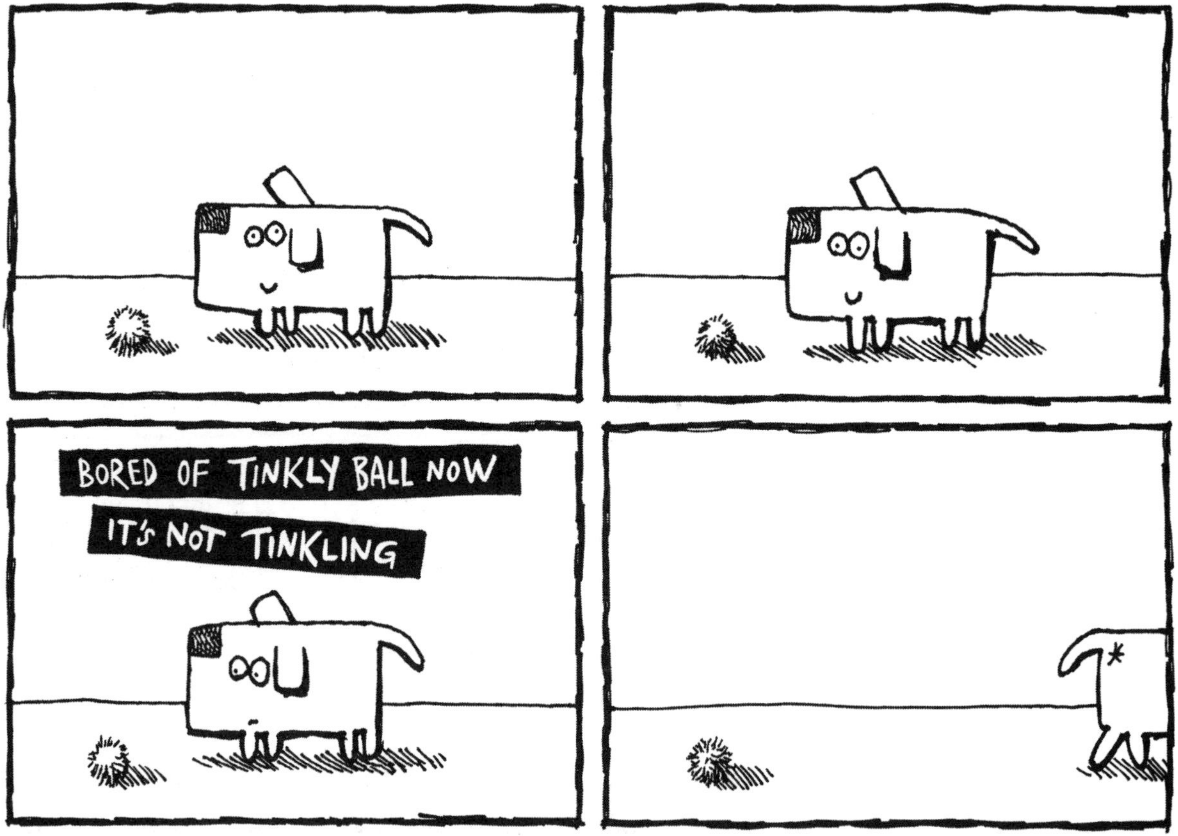
BORED OF TINKLY BALL NOW
IT'S NOT TINKLING
*

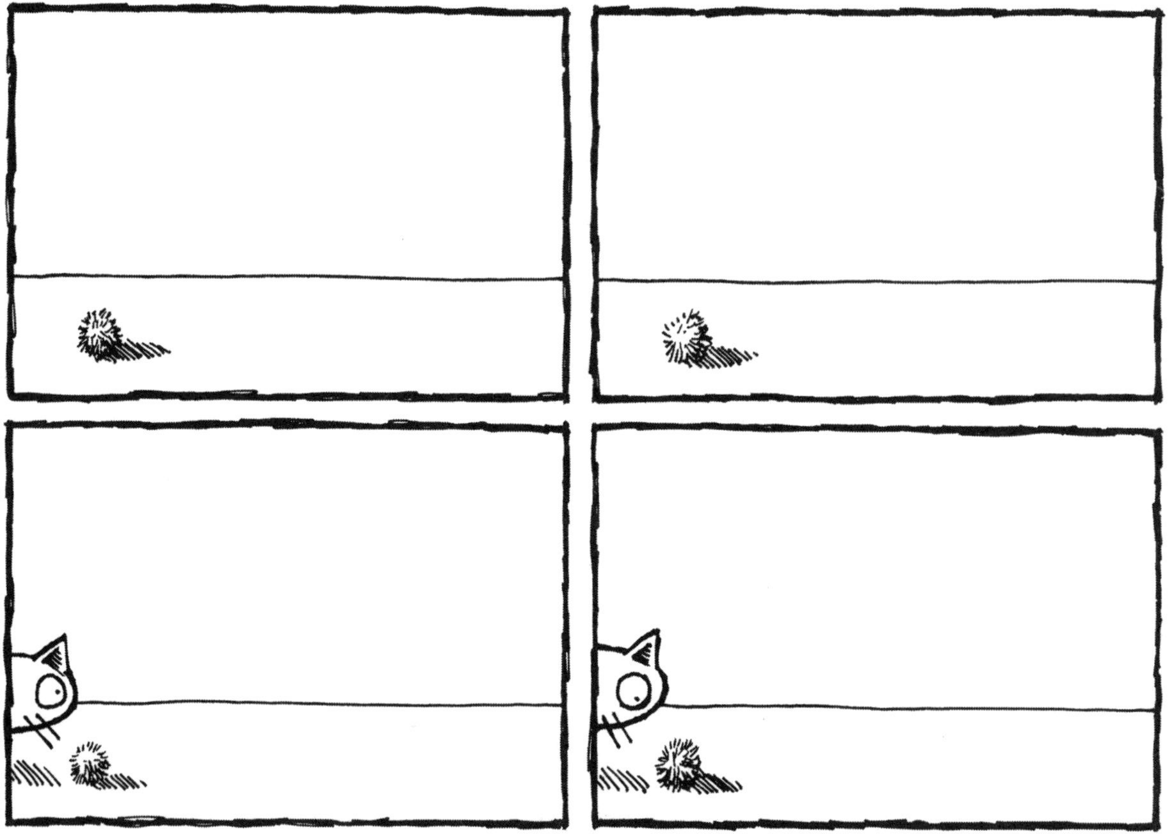

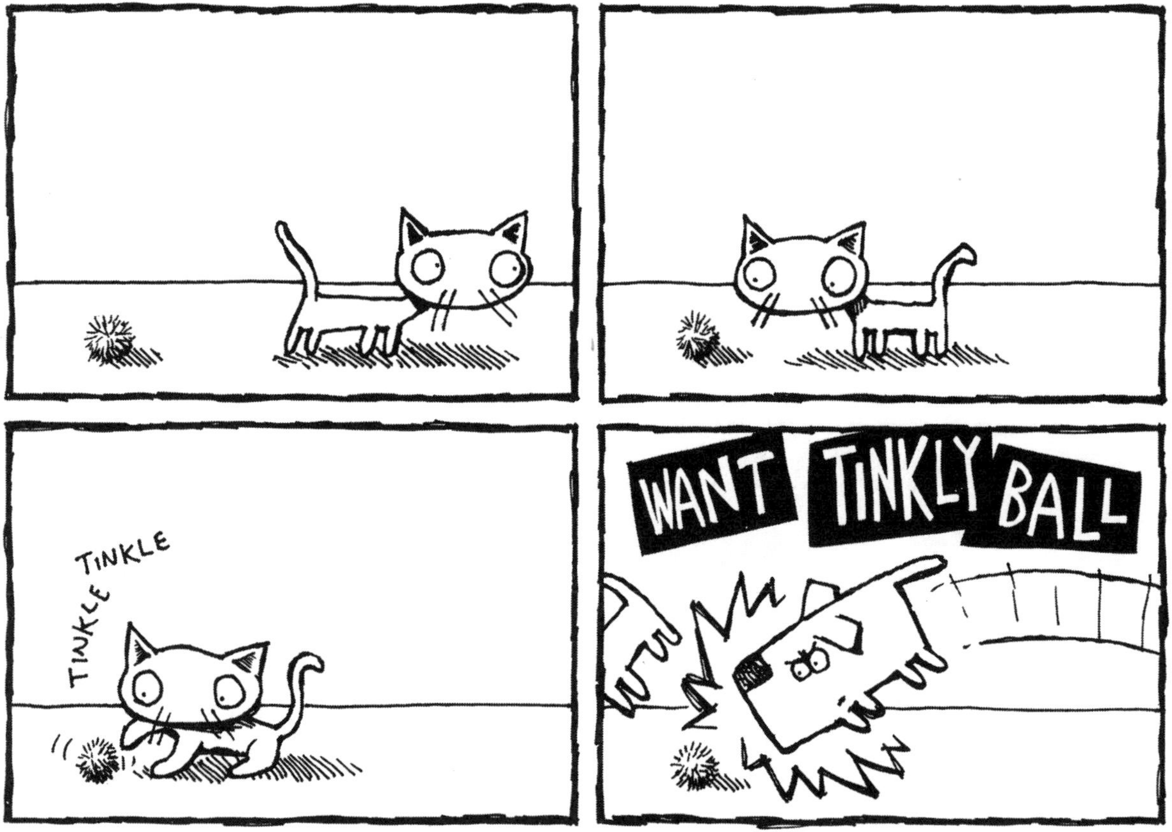
TINKLE
TINKLE
WANT TINKLY BALL

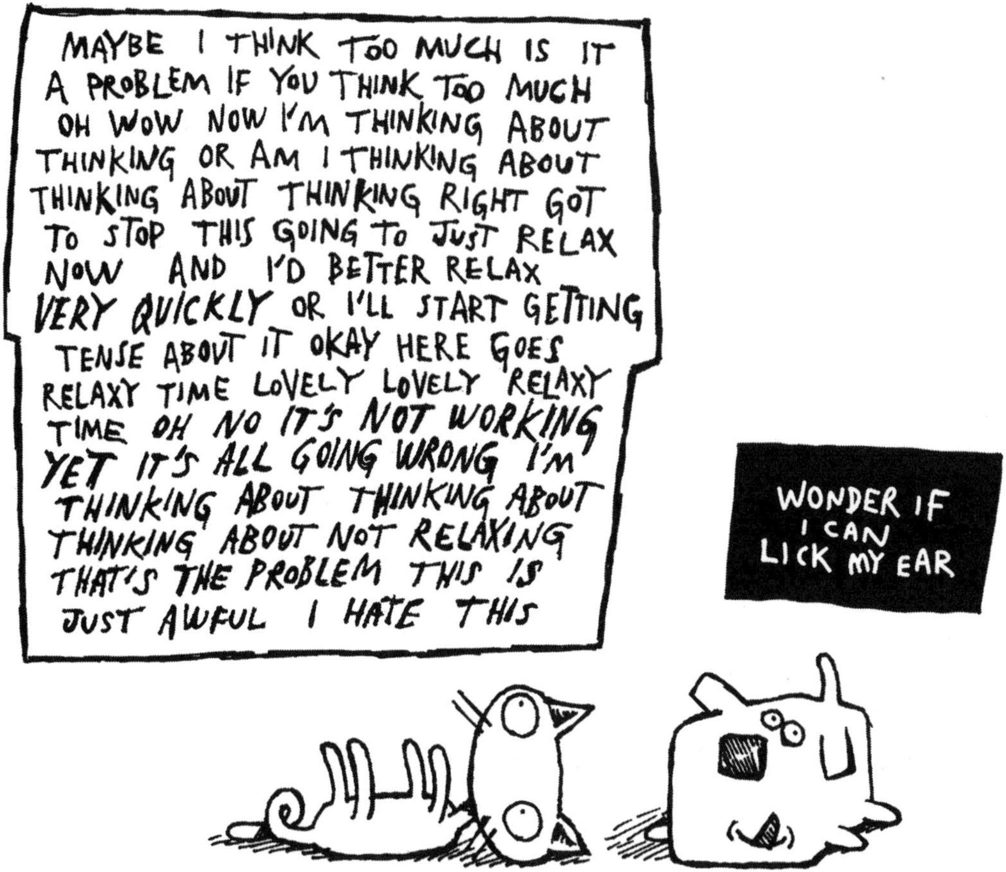
MAYBE I THINK TOO MUCH IS IT A PROBLEM IF YOU THINK TOO MUCH OH WOW NOW I'M THINKING ABOUT THINKING OR AM I THINKING ABOUT THINKING ABOUT THINKING RIGHT GOT TO STOP THIS GOING TO JUST RELAX NOW AND I'D BETTER RELAX VERY QUICKLY OR I'LL START GETTING TENSE ABOUT IT OKAY HERE GOES RELAXY TIME LOVELY LOVELY RELAXY TIME OH NO IT'S NOT WORKING YET IT'S ALL GOING WRONG I'M THINKING ABOUT THINKING ABOUT THINKING ABOUT NOT RELAXING THAT'S THE PROBLEM THIS IS JUST AWFUL I HATE THIS
WONDER IF I CAN LICK MY EAR

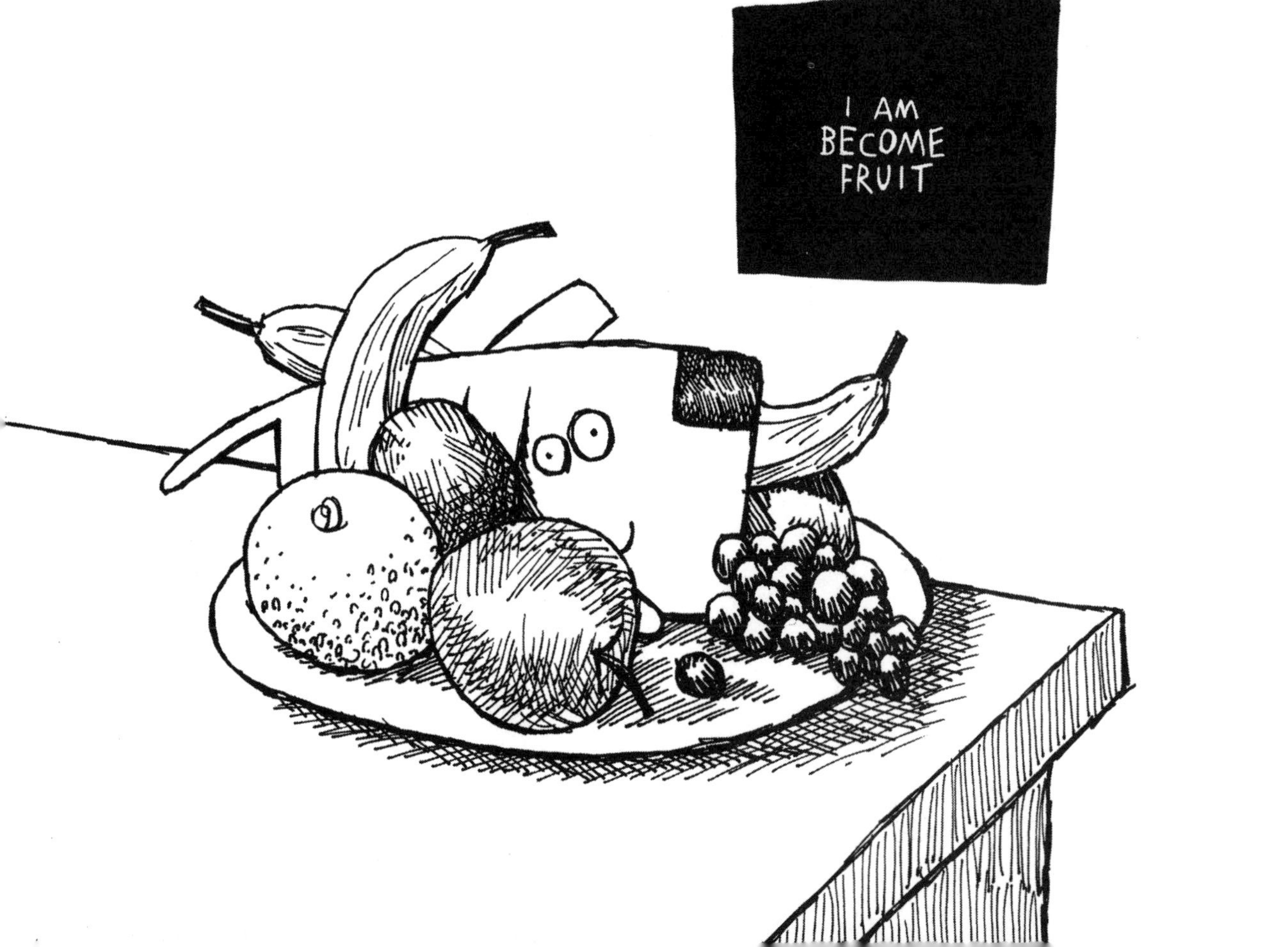
I AM
BECOME
FRUIT

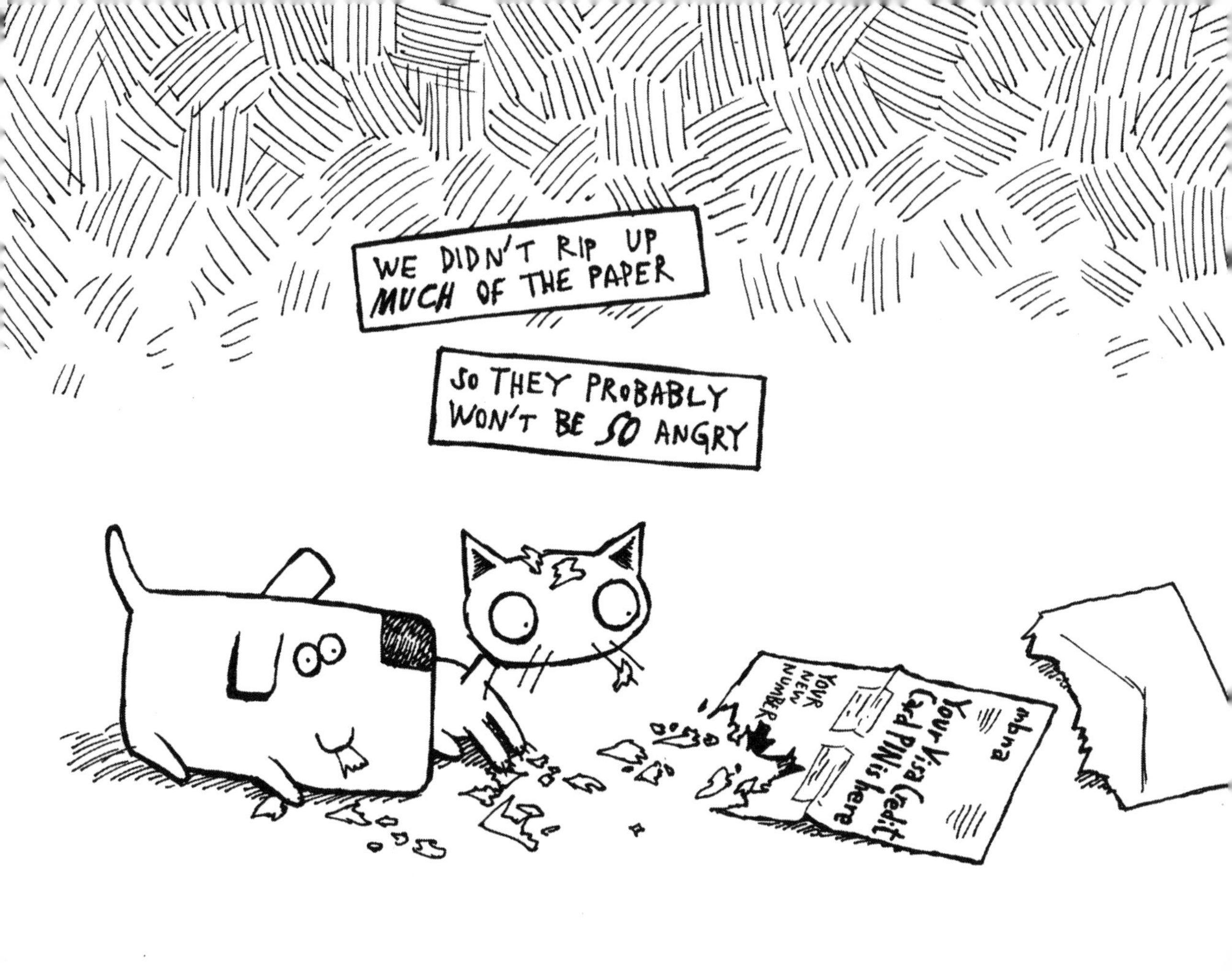
WE DIDN'T RIP UP MUCH OF THE PAPER
SO THEY PROBABLY WON'T BE SO ANGRY
mbna
Your Visa Credit Card PIN is here
YOUR NEW NUMBER

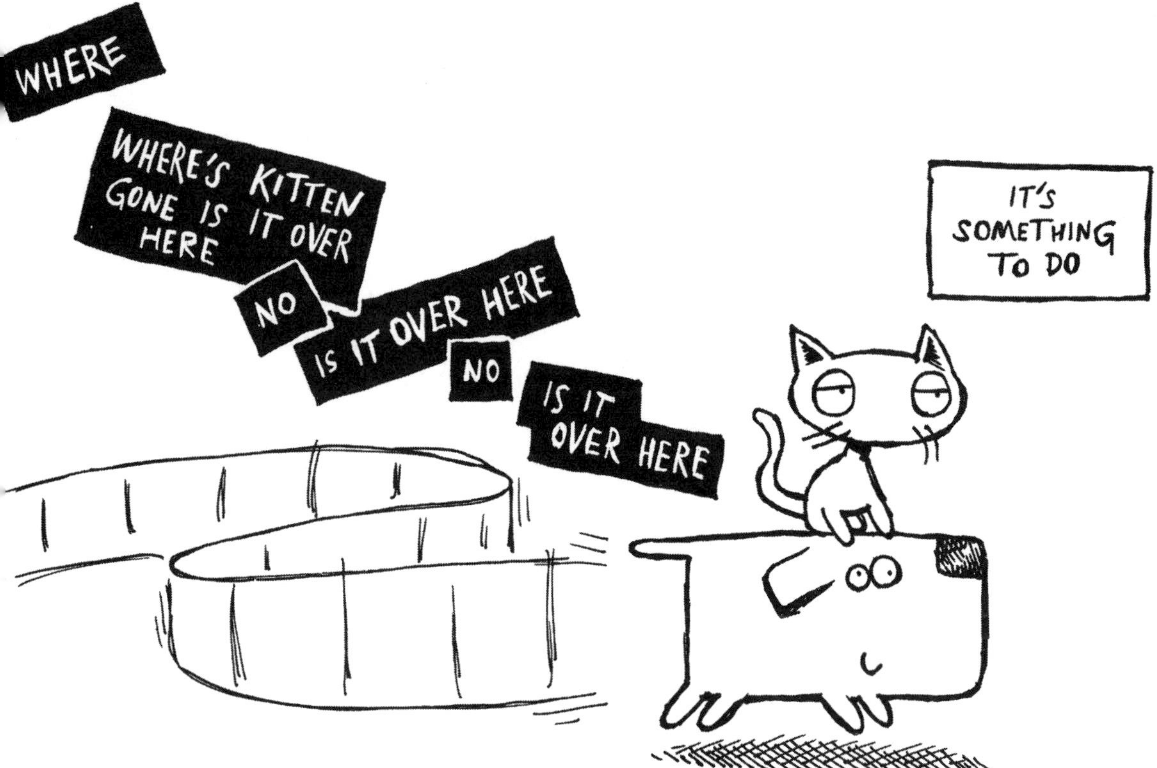
WHERE
WHERE'S KITTEN GONE IS IT OVER HERE
NO
IS IT OVER HERE
NO
IS IT OVER HERE
IT'S SOMETHING TO DO

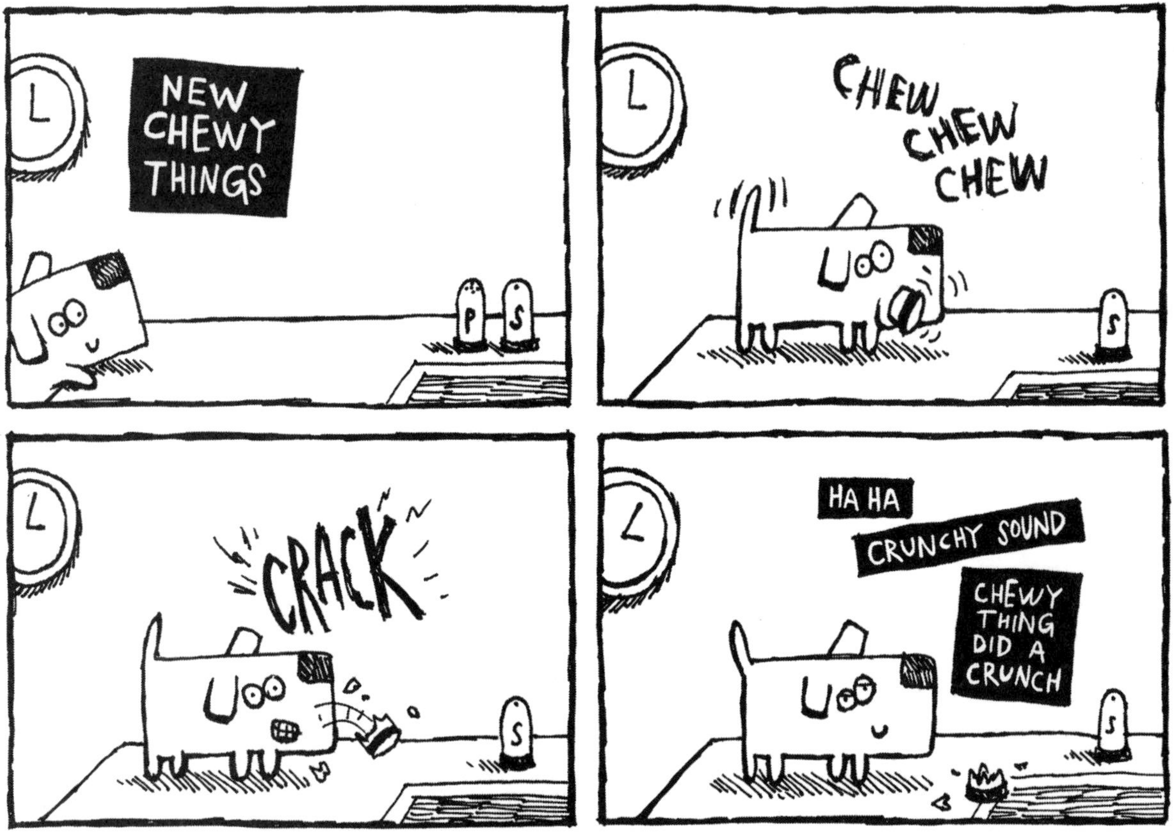
NEW CHEWY THINGS
CHEW CHEW CHEW
CRACK
HA HA
CRUNCHY SOUND
CHEWY THING DID A CRUNCH

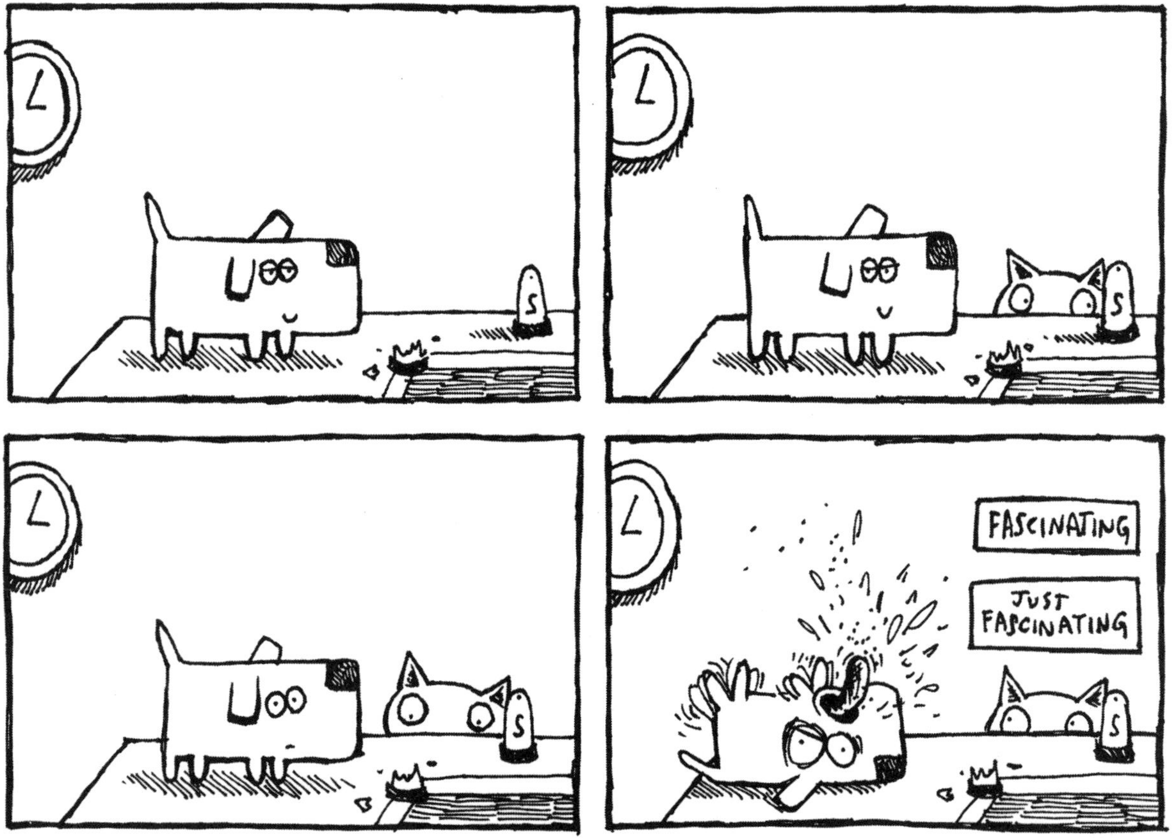

FASCINATING
JUST FASCINATING

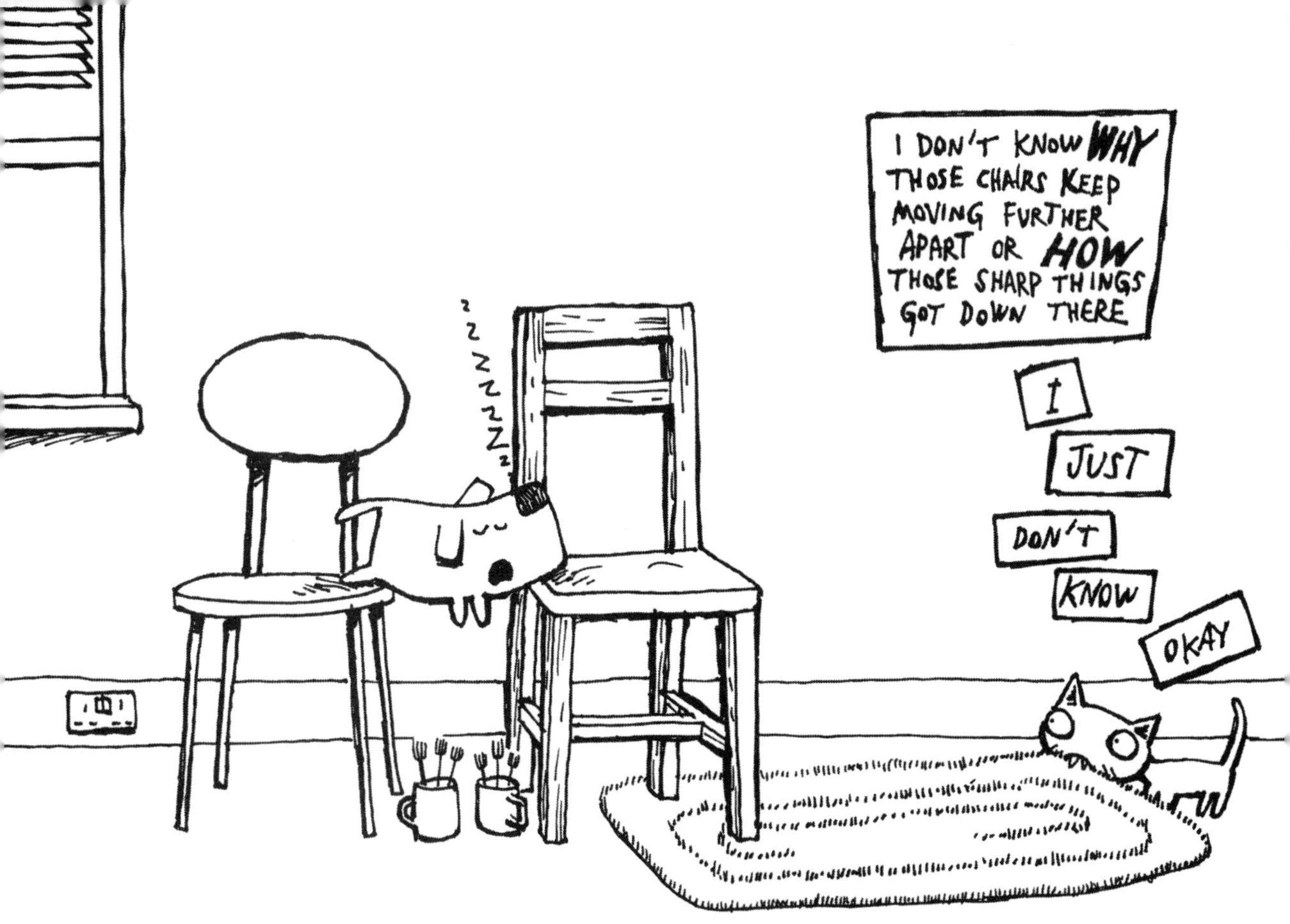
I DON'T KNOW WHY THOSE CHAIRS KEEP MOVING FURTHER APART OR HOW THOSE SHARP THINGS GOT DOWN THERE
I
JUST
DON'T
KNOW
OKAY

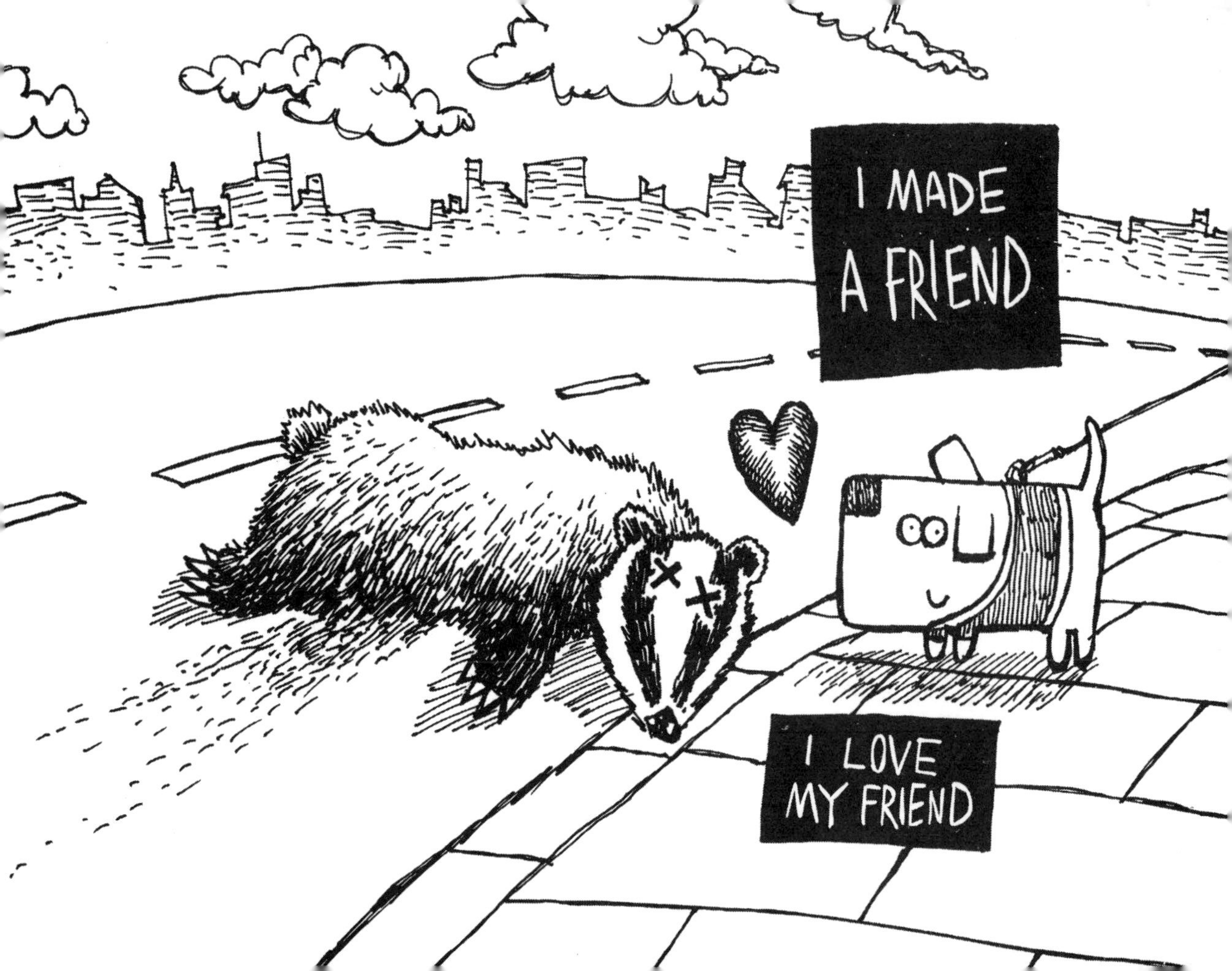
I MADE
A FRIEND
I LOVE
MY FRIEND

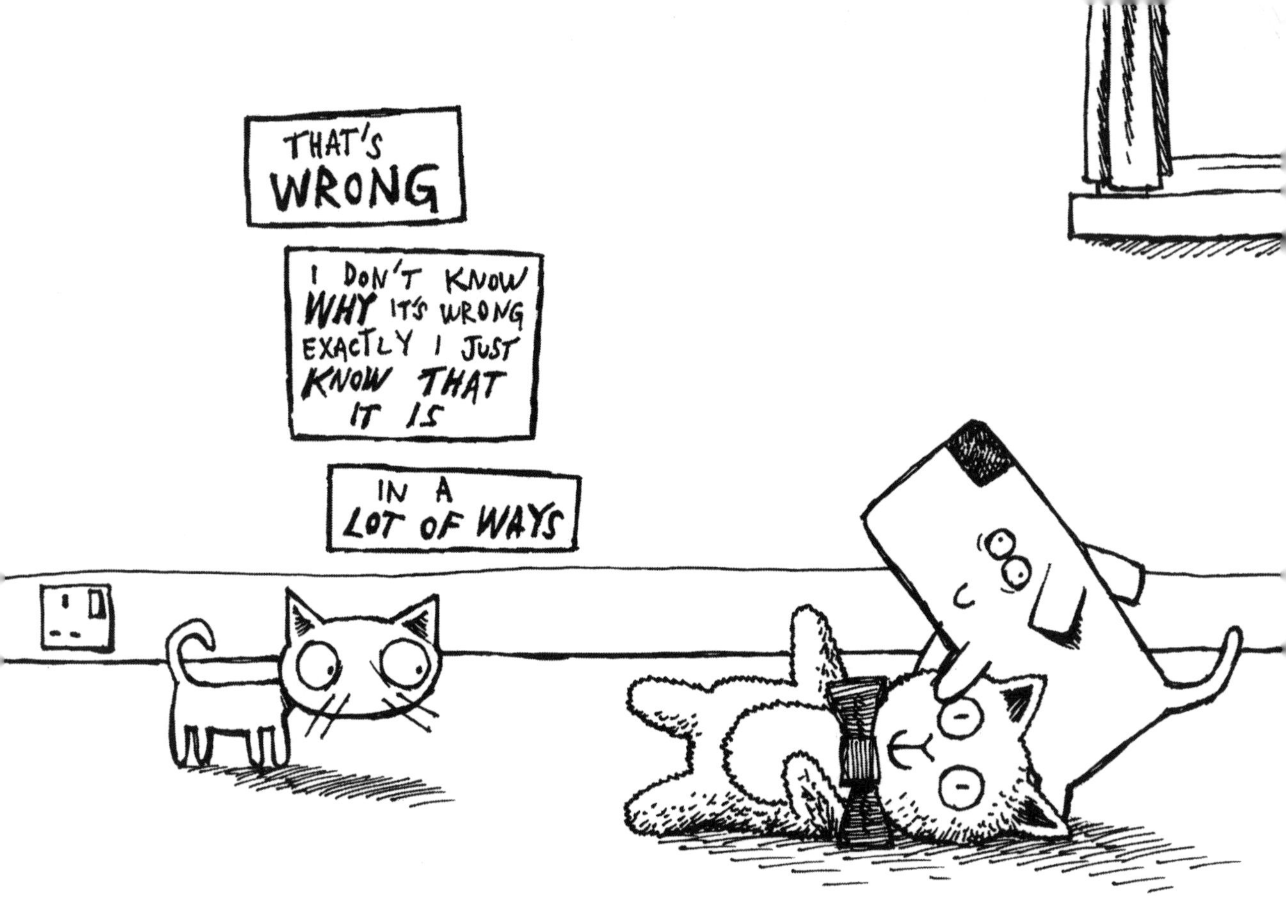
THAT'S WRONG
I DON'T KNOW WHY IT'S WRONG EXACTLY I JUST KNOW THAT IT IS
IN A LOT OF WAYS

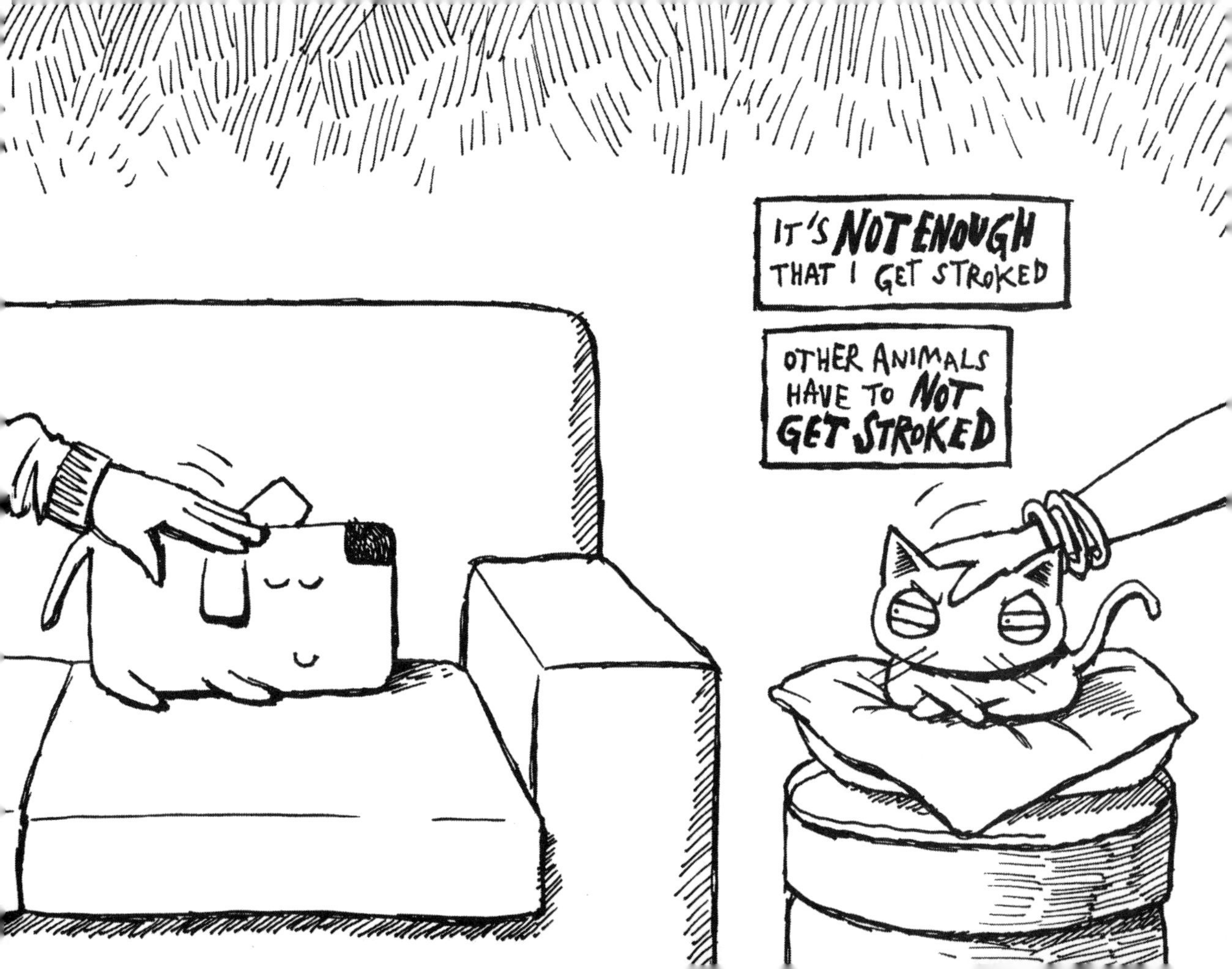
IT'S NOT ENOUGH THAT I GET STROKED
OTHER ANIMALS HAVE TO NOT GET STROKED

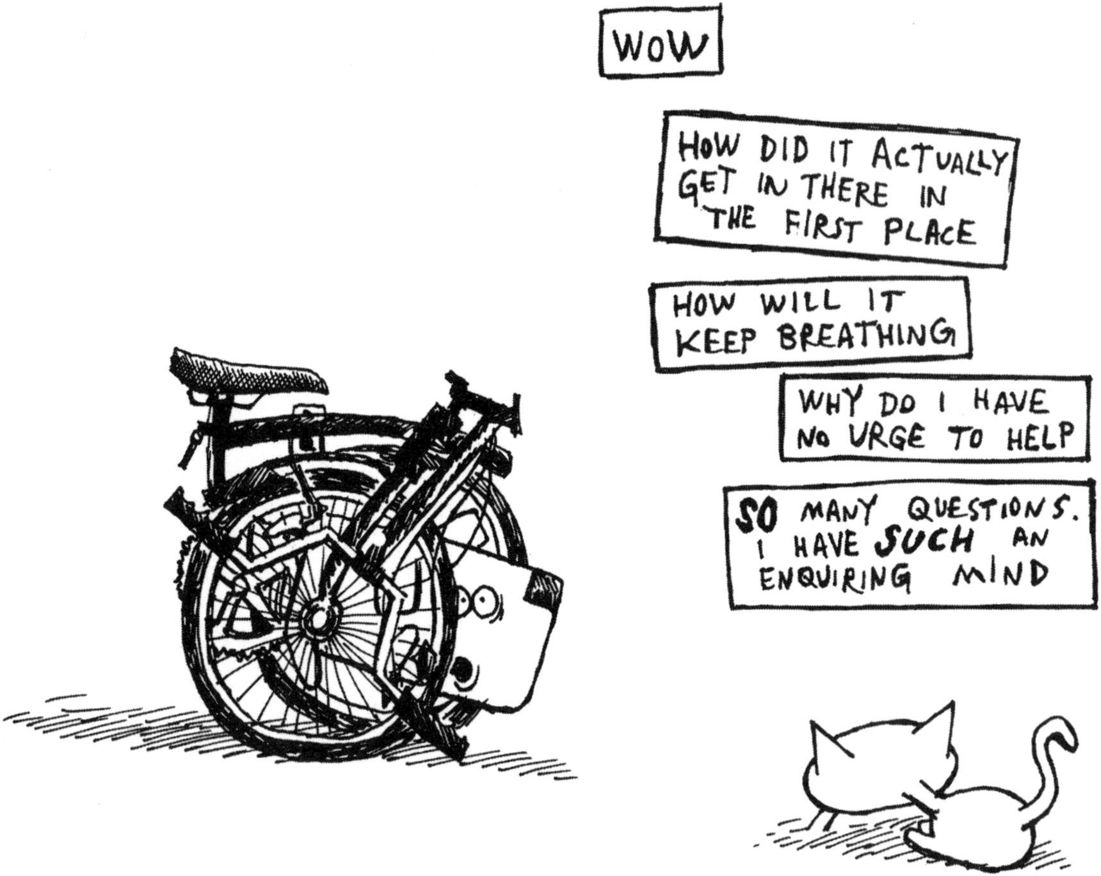
WOW
HOW DID IT ACTUALLY GET IN THERE IN THE FIRST PLACE
HOW WILL IT KEEP BREATHING
WHY DO I HAVE NO URGE TO HELP
SO MANY QUESTIONS. I HAVE SUCH AN ENQUIRING MIND

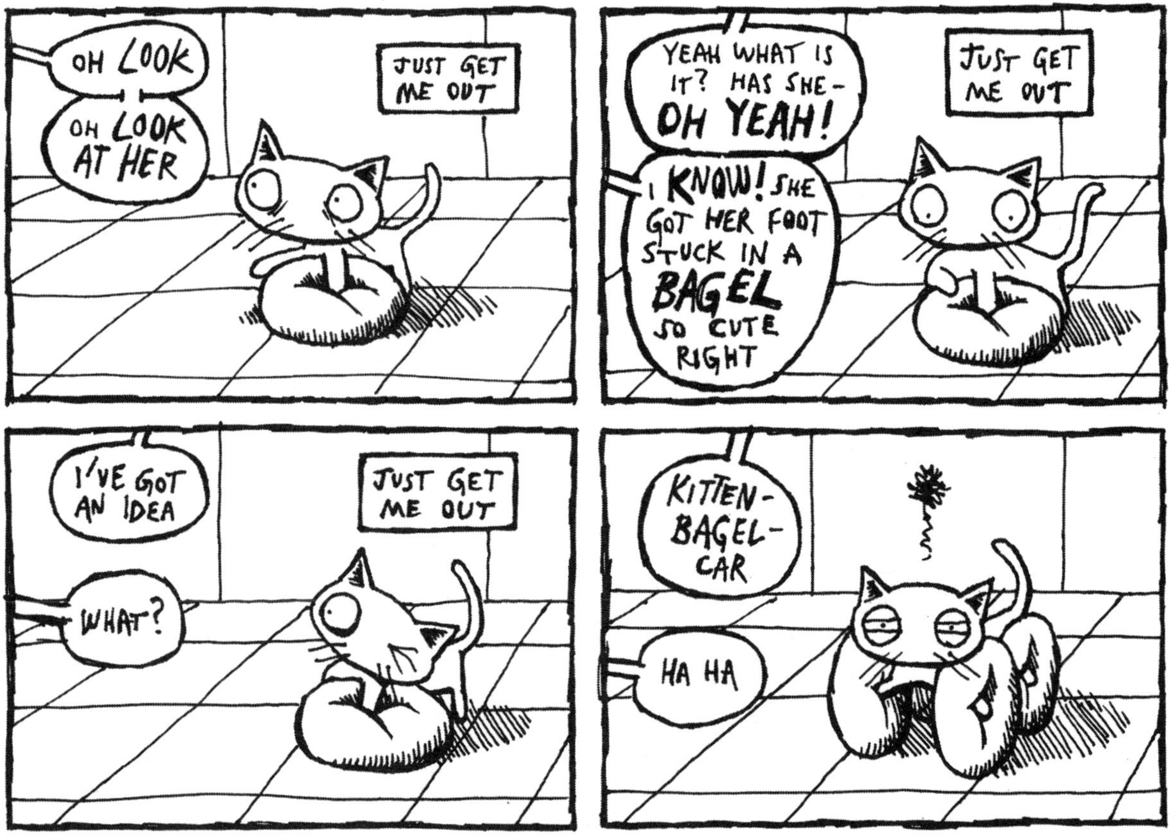
OH LOOK
OH LOOK AT HER
JUST GET ME OUT
YEAH WHAT IS IT? HAS SHE- OH YEAH!
I KNOW! SHE GOT HER FOOT STUCK IN A BAGEL SO CUTE RIGHT
JUST GET ME OUT
I'VE GOT AN IDEA
WHAT?
JUST GET ME OUT
KITTEN-BAGEL-CAR
HA HA

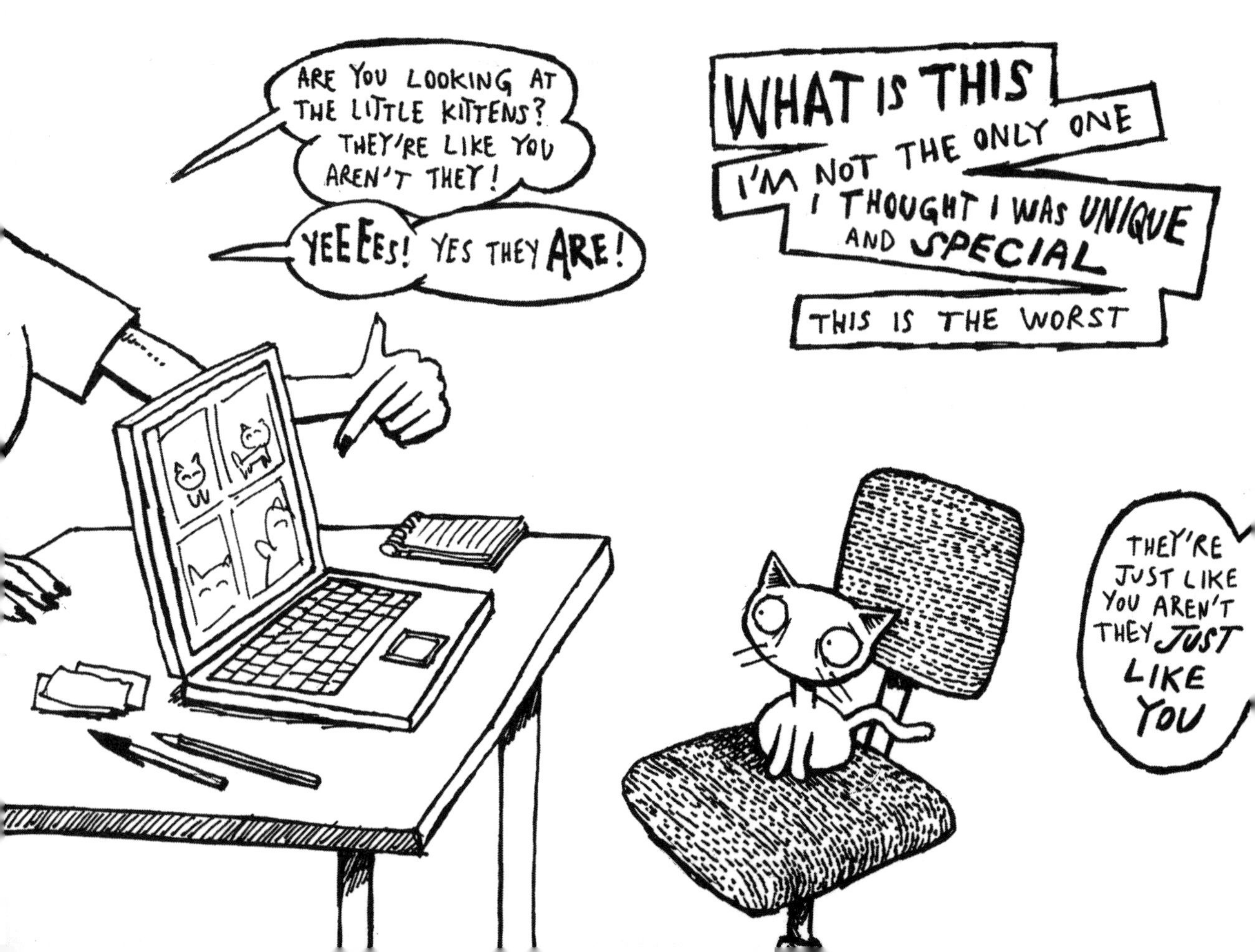
ARE YOU LOOKING AT THE LITTLE KITTENS? THEY'RE LIKE YOU AREN'T THEY!
YEEEES! YES THEY ARE!
WHAT IS THIS
I'M NOT THE ONLY ONE
I THOUGHT I WAS UNIQUE AND SPECIAL
THIS IS THE WORST
THEY'RE JUST LIKE YOU AREN'T THEY JUST LIKE YOU

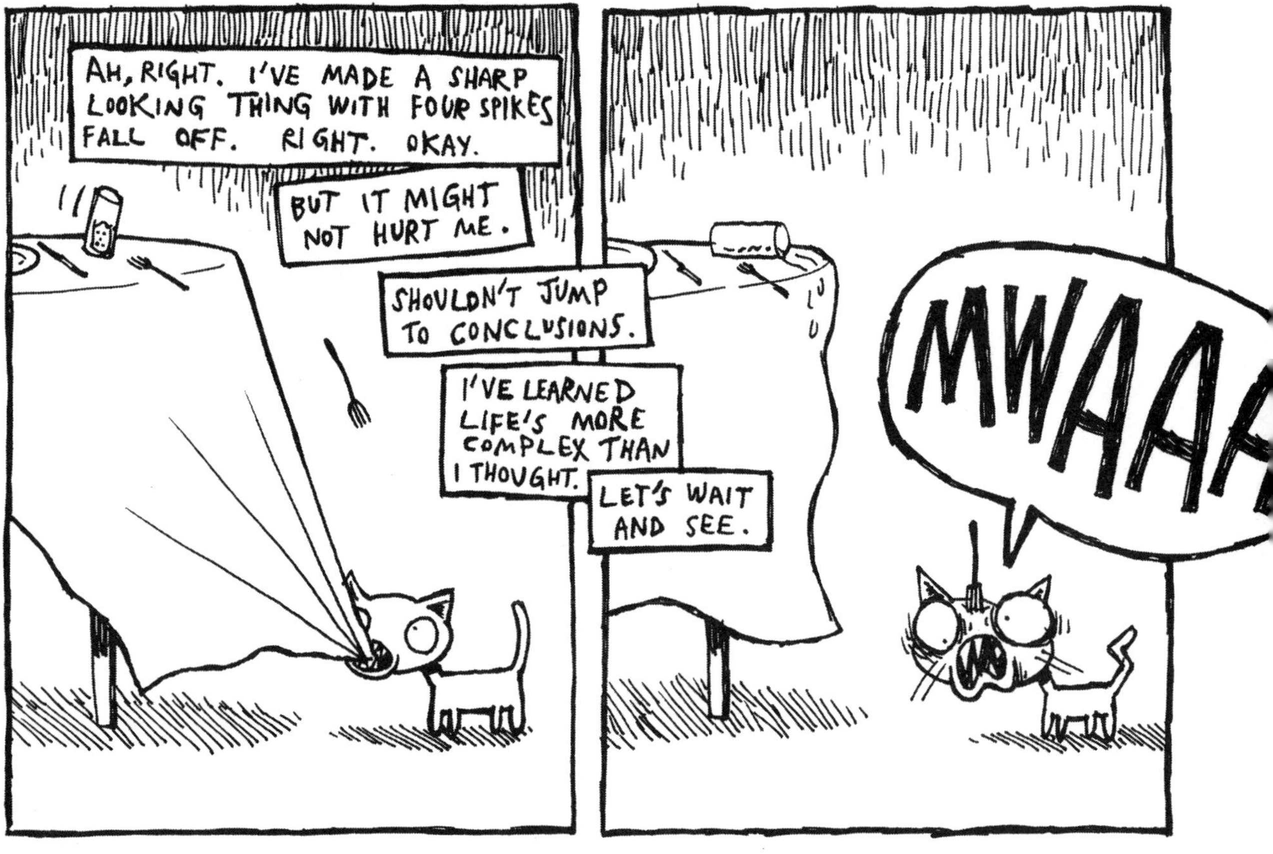
AH, RIGHT. I'VE MADE A SHARP LOOKING THING WITH FOUR SPIKES FALL OFF. RIGHT. OKAY.
BUT IT MIGHT NOT HURT ME.
SHOULDN'T JUMP TO CONCLUSIONS.
I'VE LEARNED LIFE'S MORE COMPLEX THAN I THOUGHT.
LET'S WAIT AND SEE.
MWAAA

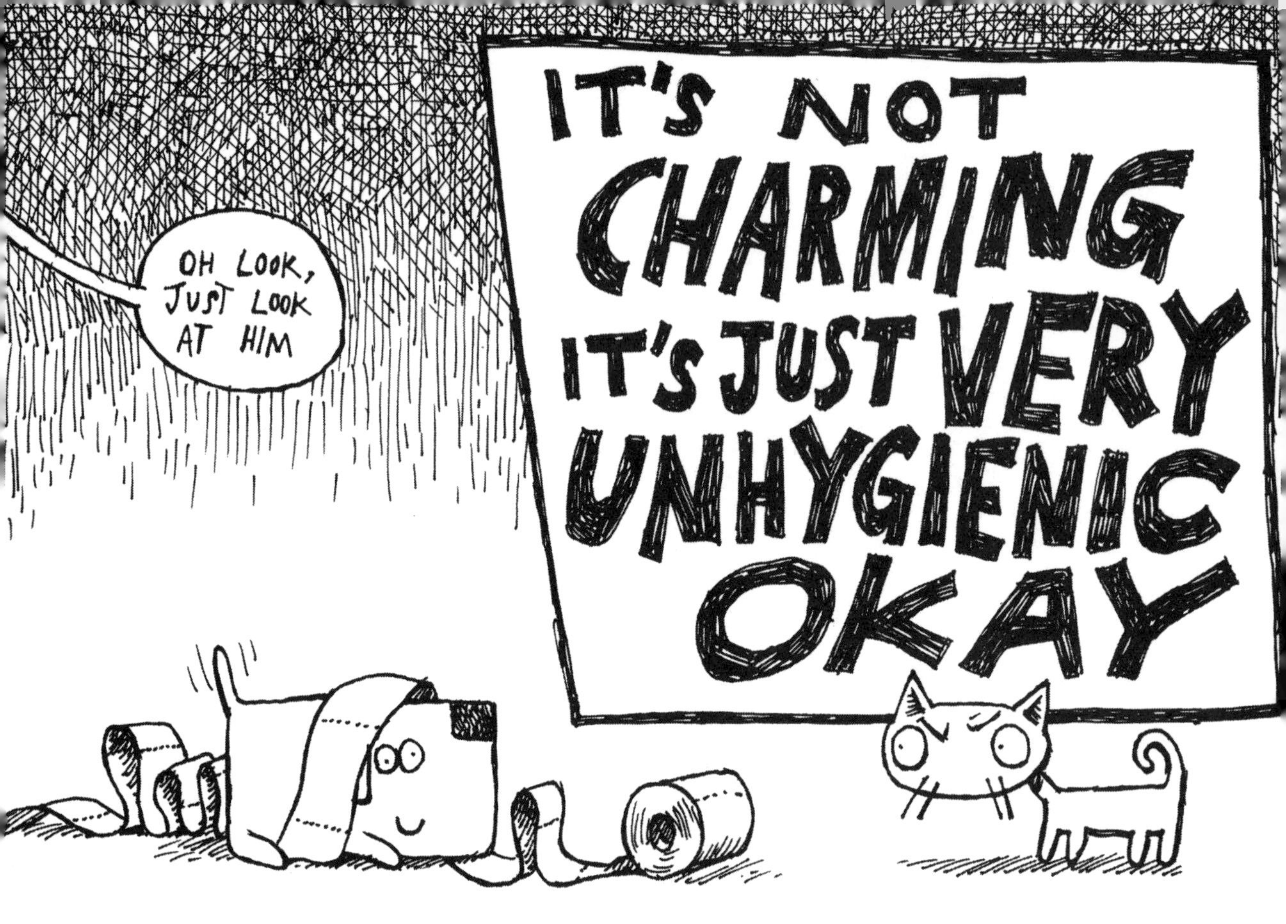
OH LOOK, JUST LOOK AT HIM
IT'S NOT CHARMING IT'S JUST VERY UNHYGIENIC OKAY

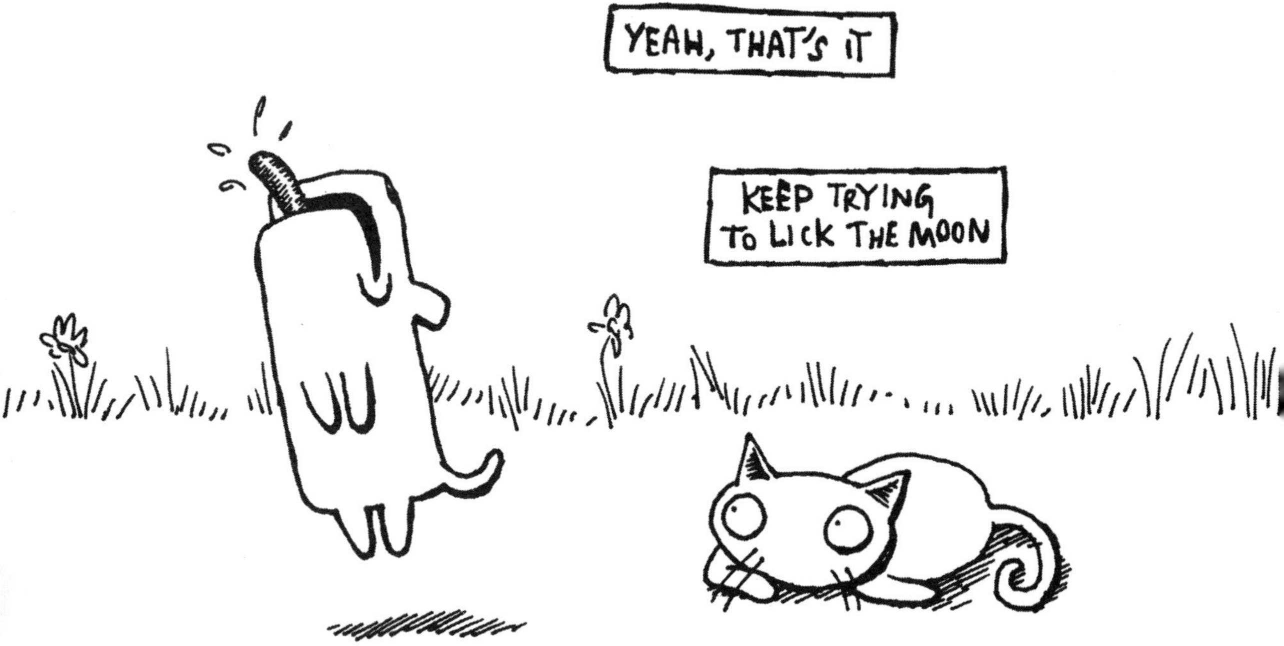
YEAH, THAT'S IT
KEEP TRYING TO LICK THE MOON

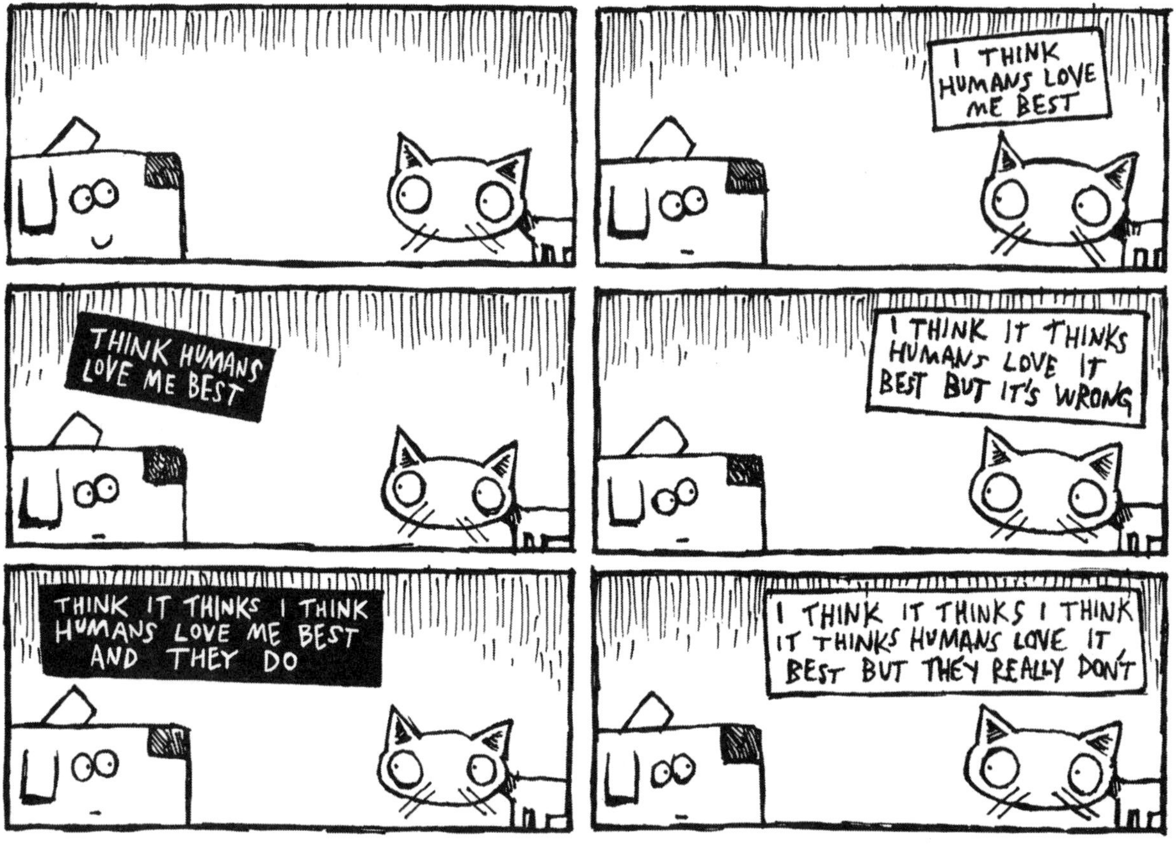
I THINK HUMANS LOVE ME BEST
THINK HUMANS LOVE ME BEST
I THINK IT THINKS HUMANS LOVE IT BEST BUT IT'S WRONG
THINK IT THINKS I THINK HUMANS LOVE ME BEST AND THEY DO
I THINK IT THINKS I THINK IT THINKS HUMANS LOVE IT BEST BUT THEY REALLY DON'T

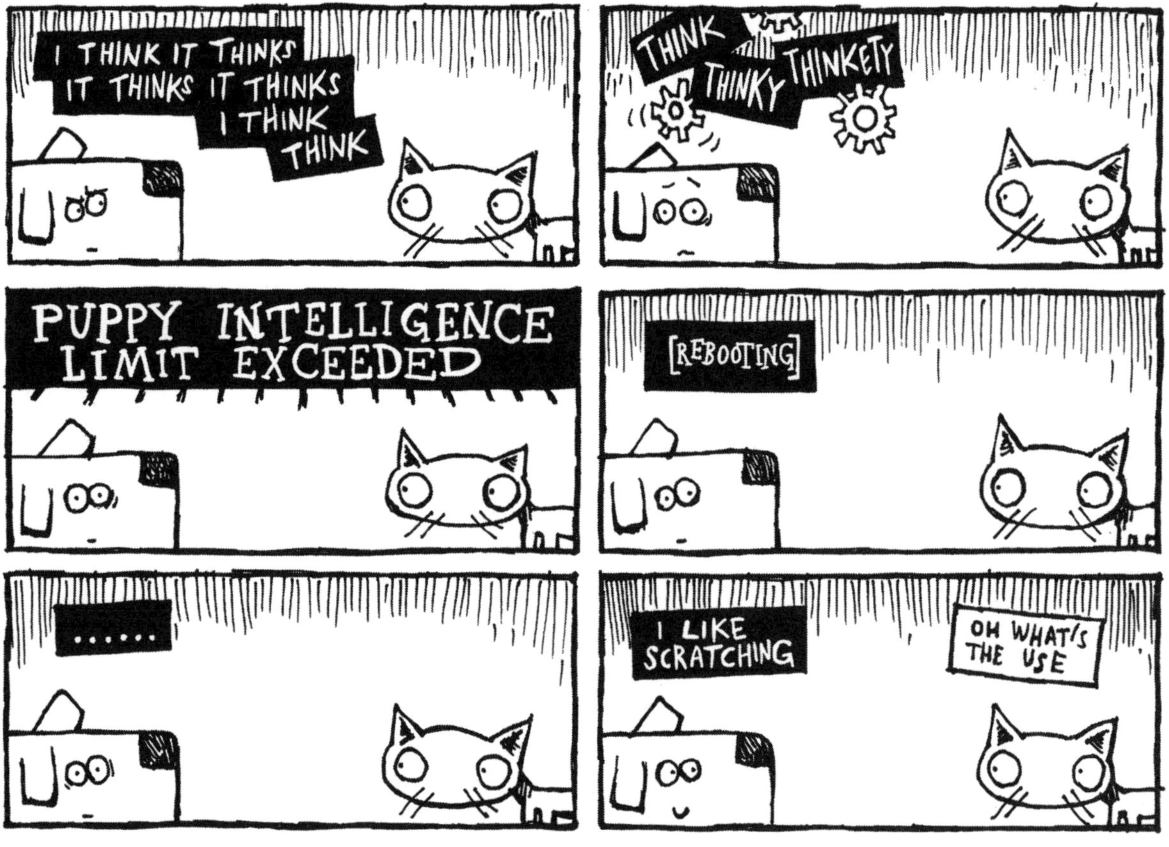
I THINK IT THINKS IT THINKS IT THINKS I THINK THINK
THINK
THINKY
THINKETY
PUPPY INTELLIGENCE LIMIT EXCEEDED
[REBOOTING]
....
I LIKE SCRATCHING
OH WHAT'S THE USE

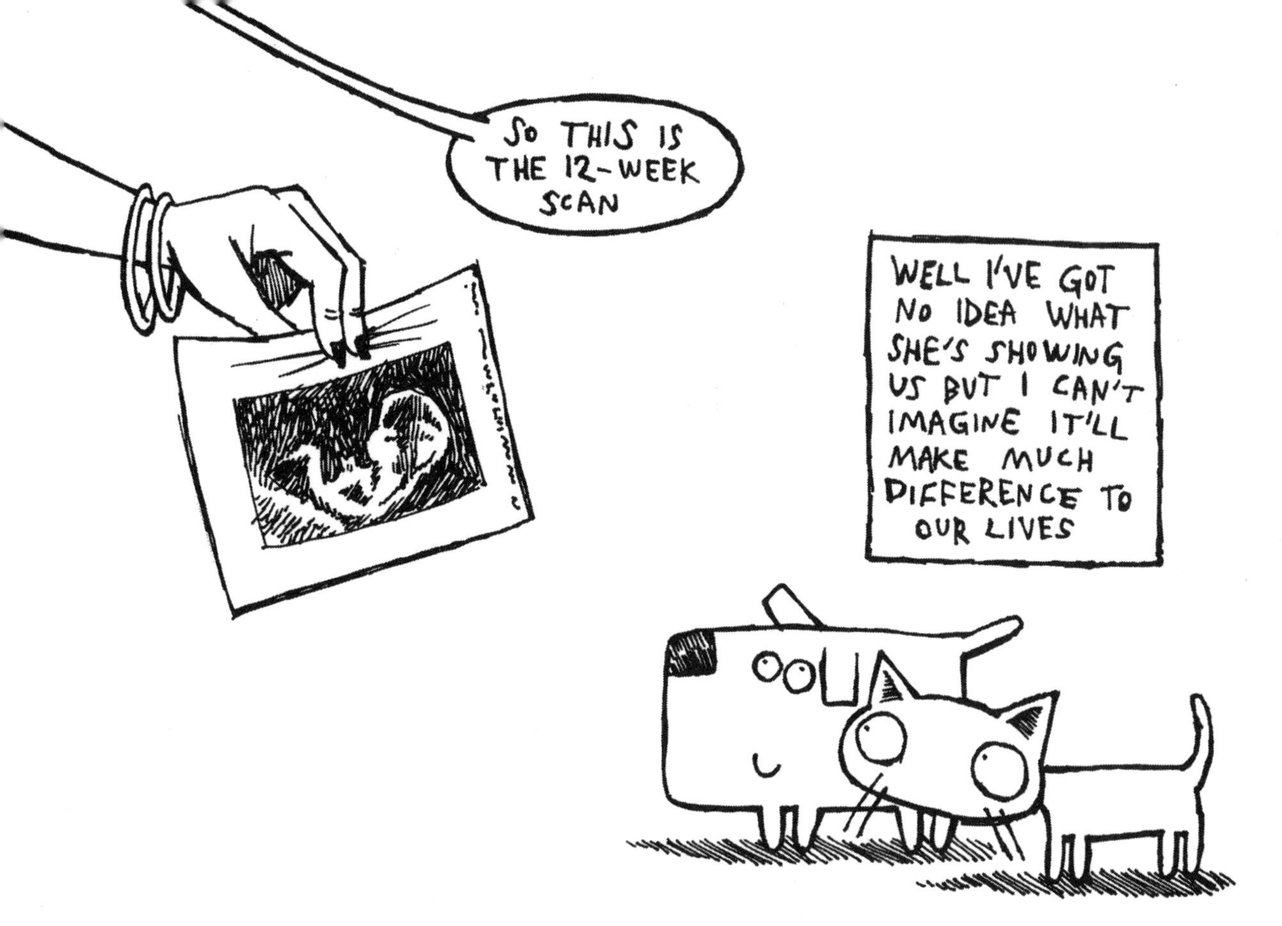
SO THIS IS THE 12-WEEK SCAN
WELL I'VE GOT NO IDEA WHAT SHE'S SHOWING US BUT I CAN'T IMAGINE IT'LL MAKE MUCH DIFFERENCE TO OUR LIVES

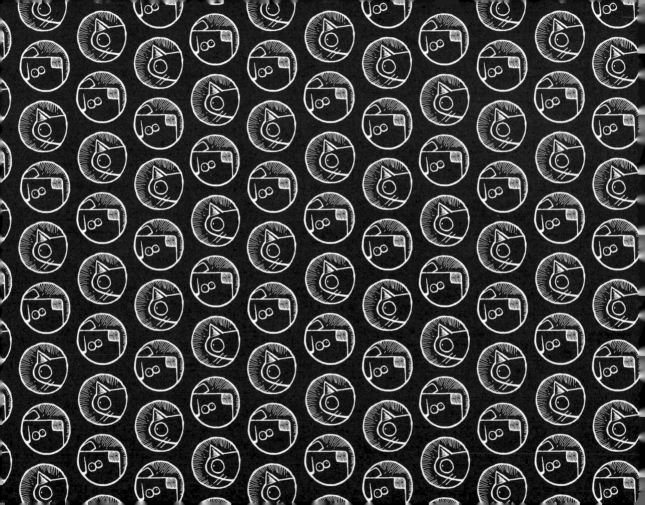